FAVORITE CHRISTMAS SONGS

ISBN 978-1-70514-006-2

Visit Hal Leonard Online at
www.halleonard.com

Contact us:
Hal Leonard
7777 West Bluemound Road
Milwaukee, WI 53213
Email: info@halleonard.com

In Europe, contact:
Hal Leonard Europe Limited
42 Wigmore Street
Marylebone, London, W1U 2RN
Email: info@halleonardeurope.com

In Australia, contact:
Hal Leonard Australia Pty. Ltd.
4 Lentara Court
Cheltenham, Victoria, 3192 Australia
Email: info@halleonard.com.au

Christmas Time Is Here
from A CHARLIE BROWN CHRISTMAS

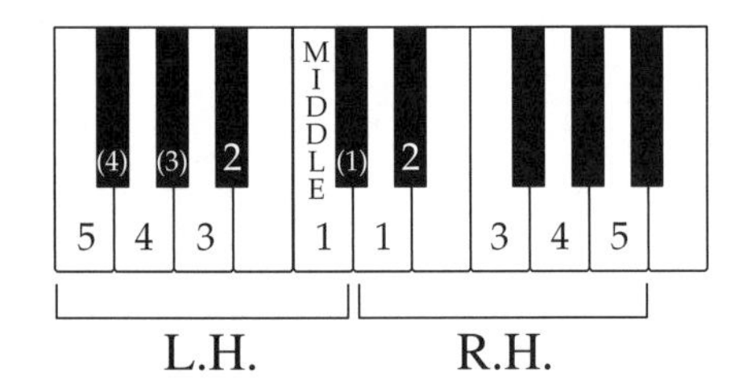

Words by Lee Mendelson
Music by Vince Guaraldi

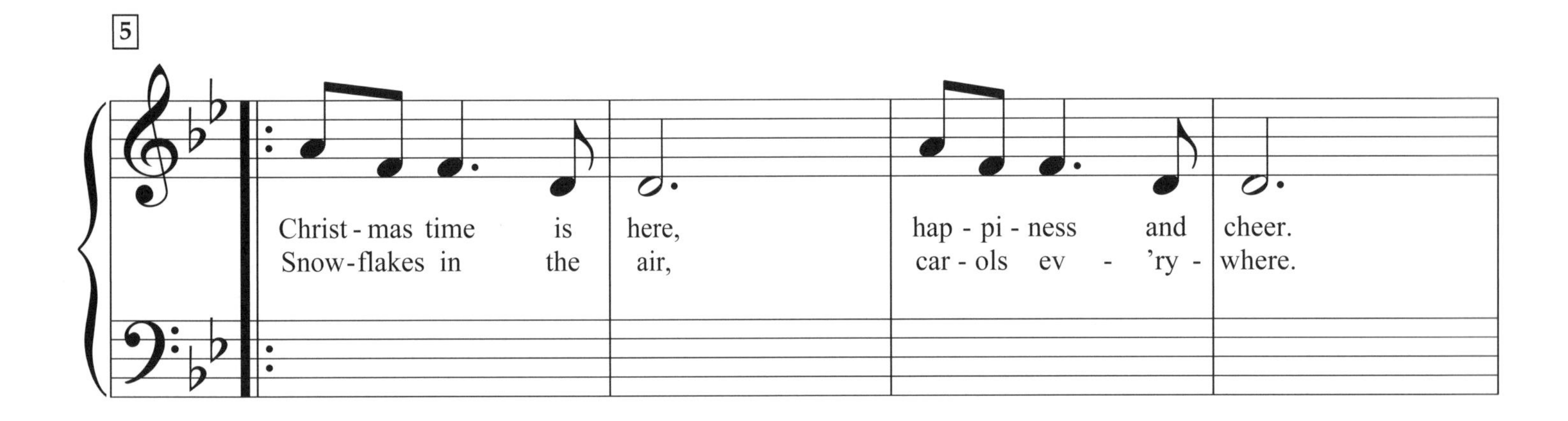

Duet Part (Student plays one octave higher than written.)

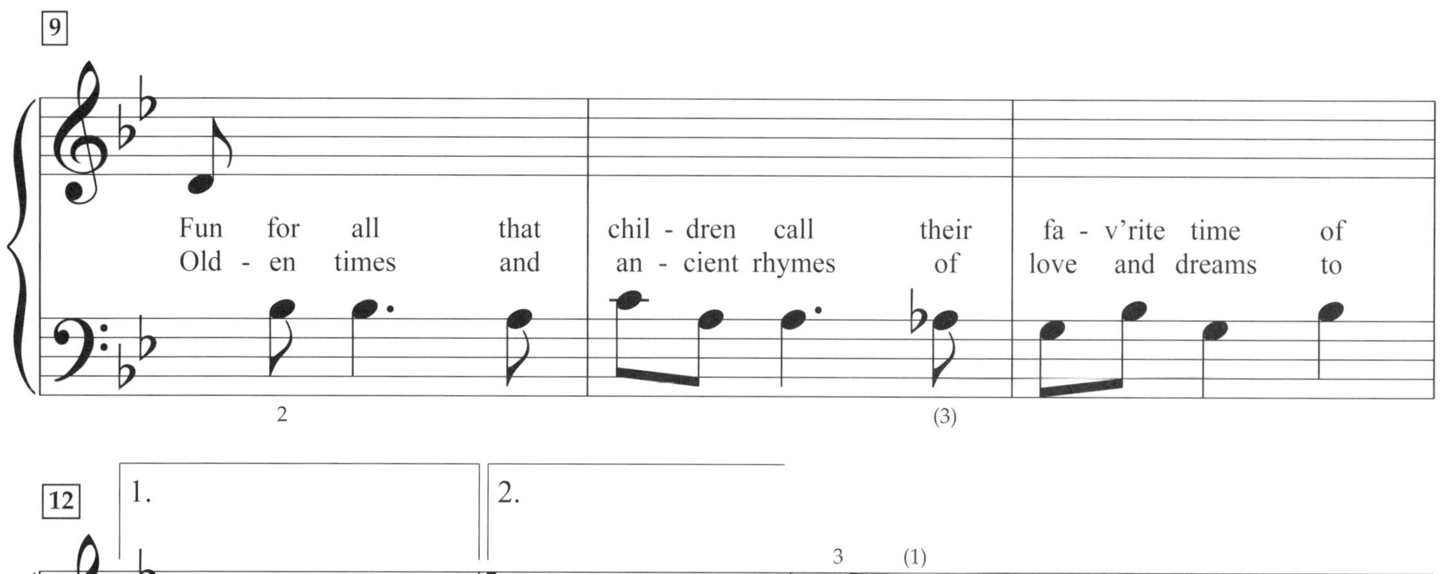
9
Fun for all that chil - dren call their fa - v'rite time of
Old - en times and an - cient rhymes of love and dreams to
2
(3)

12
1.
2.
3 (1)
year.
share.
Sleigh-bells in the air,

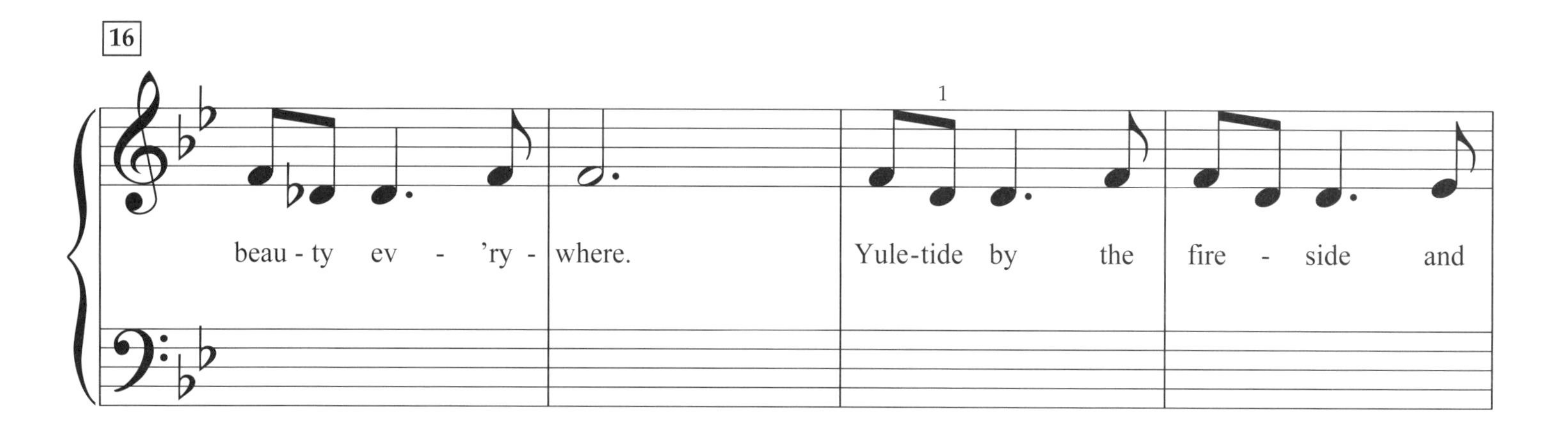
16
1
beau - ty ev - 'ry - where.
Yule-tide by the fire - side and

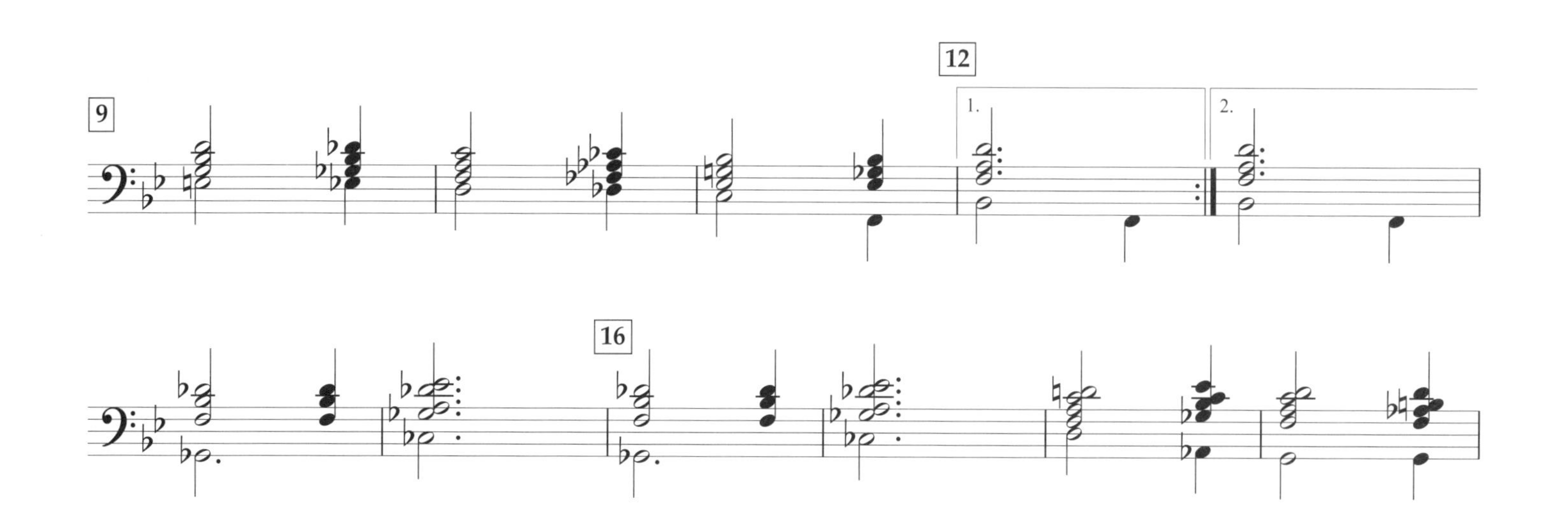
9
12
1.
2.
16

20
joy - ful mem - 'ries
there.
Christ-mas time is
here,

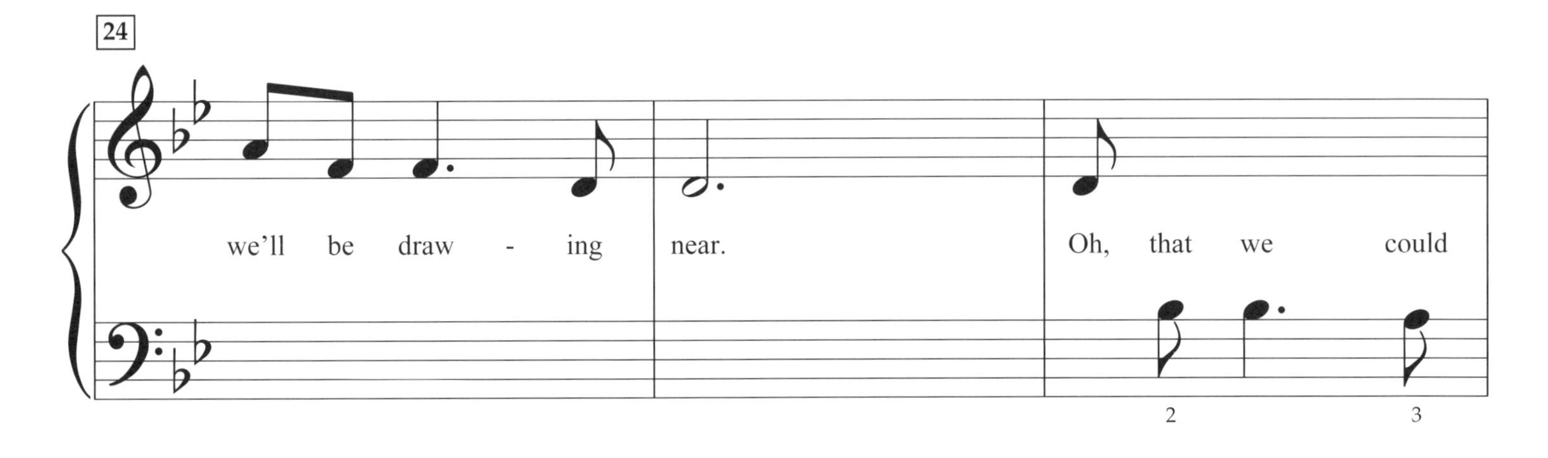
24
we'll be draw - ing
near.
Oh, that we could
2
3

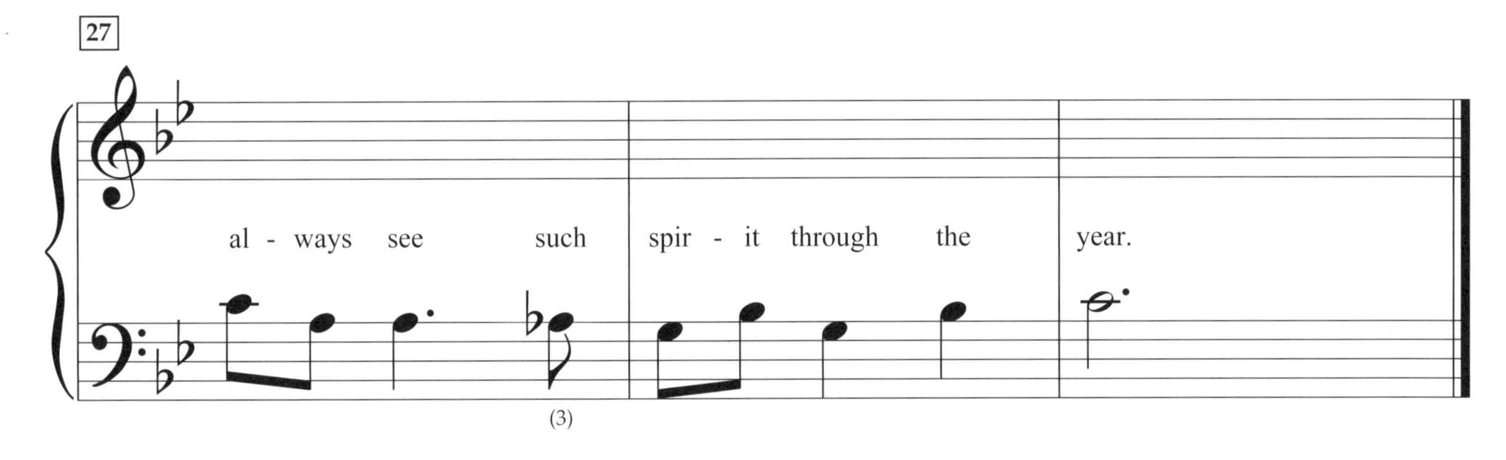
27
al - ways see such
spir - it through the
year.
(3)

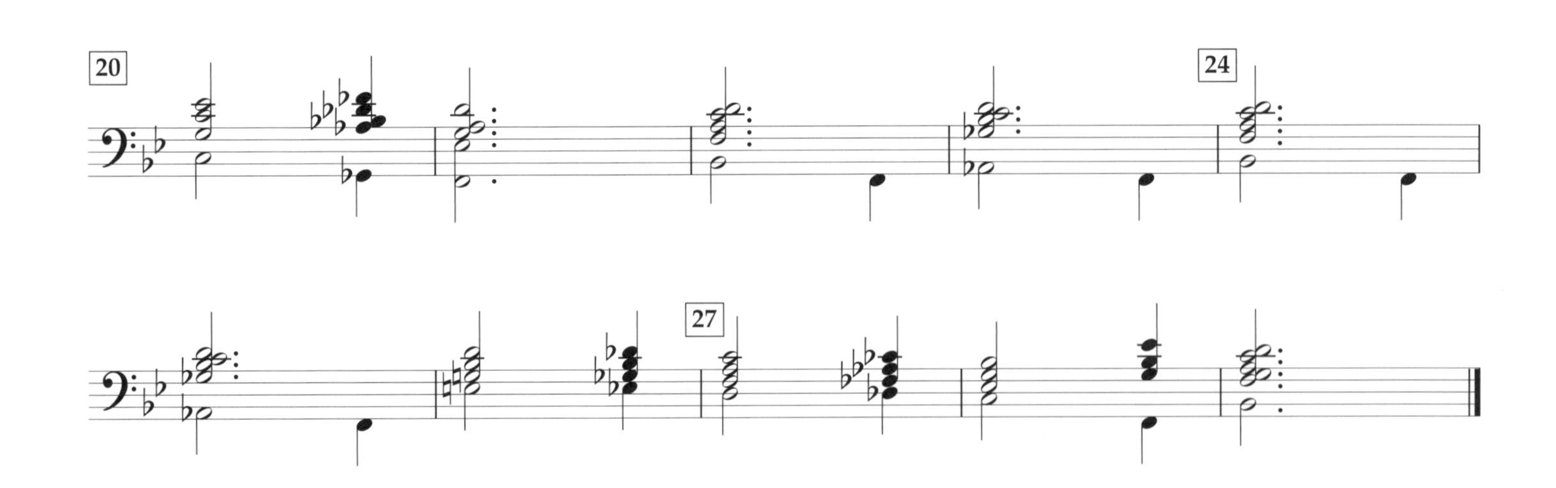
20
24
27

All I Want for Christmas Is You

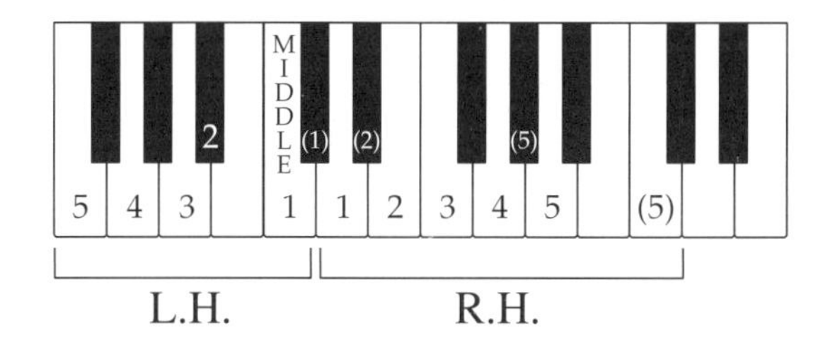

Words and Music by Mariah Carey
and Walter Afanasieff

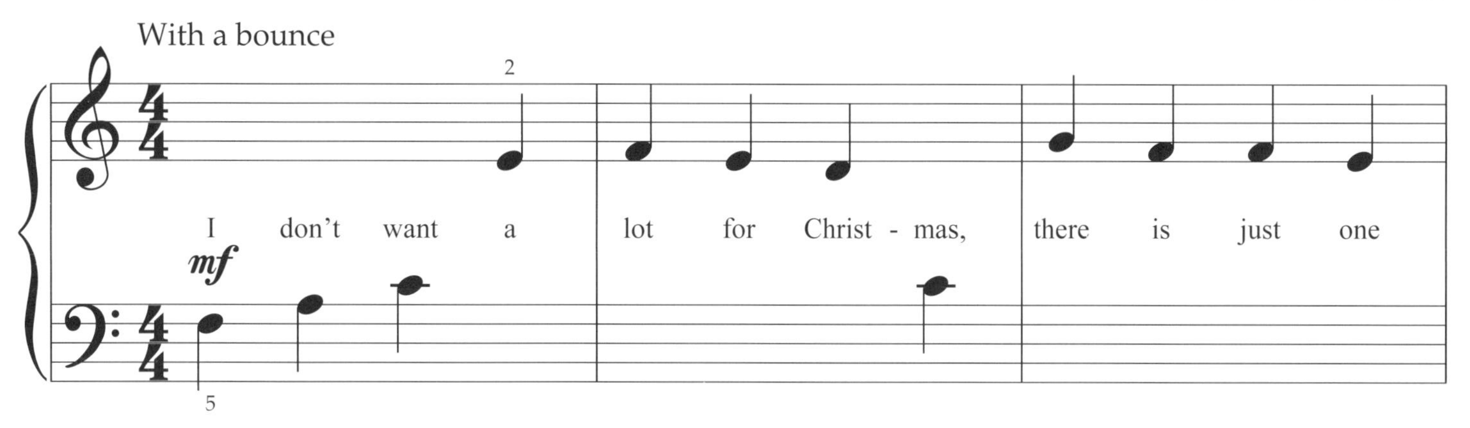

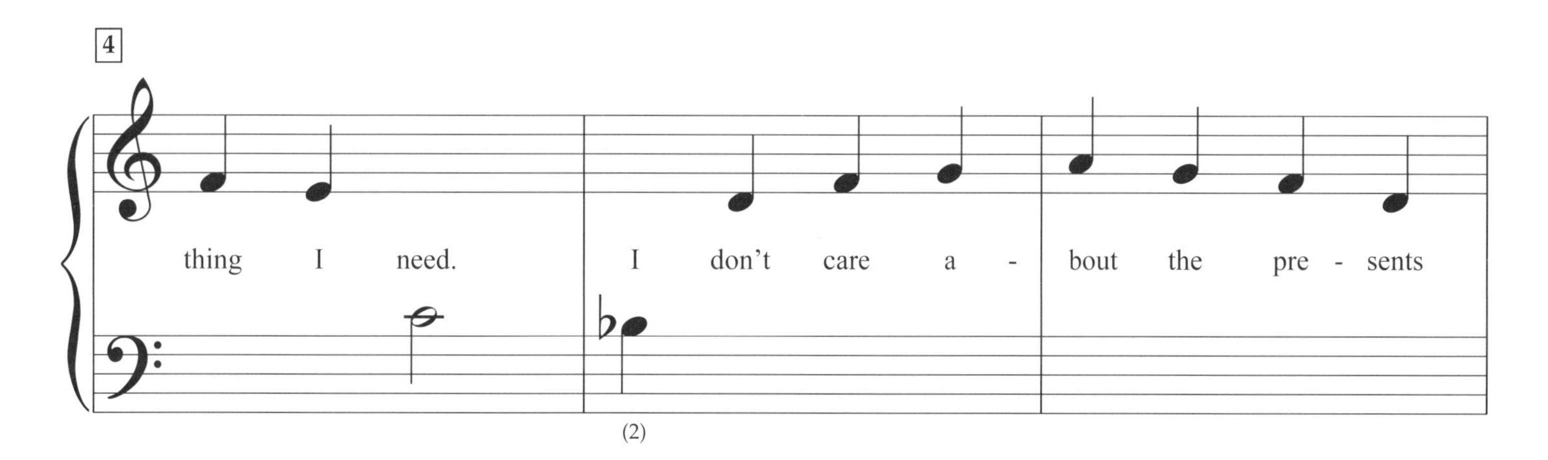

Duet Part (Student plays one octave higher than written.)

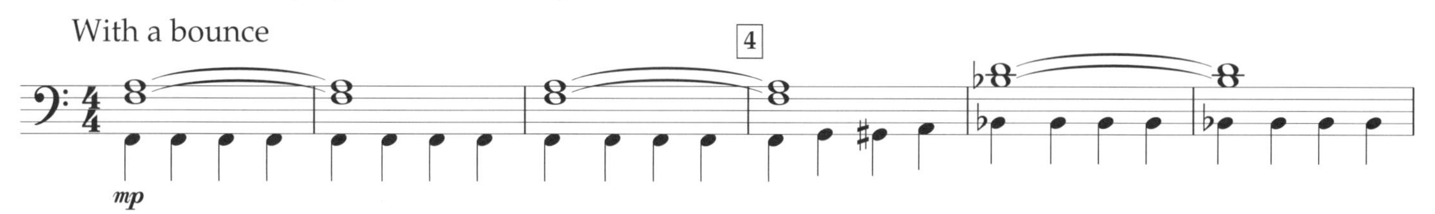

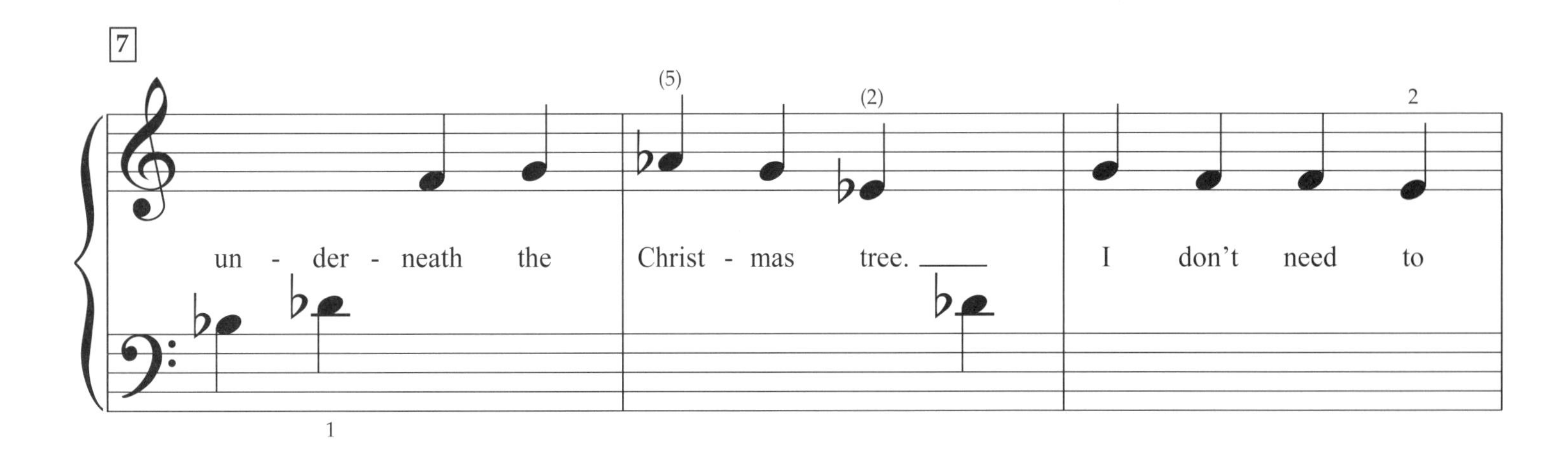
7
(5)
(2)
2
un - der - neath the Christ - mas tree. I don't need to
1

10
hang my stock - ing there up - on the fire - place.
1

13
5
San - ta Claus won't make me hap - py with a toy on
(1)

7
10
13

16
(5)
(2)
2
Christ - mas day.
I just want you
for my own,
more than you could

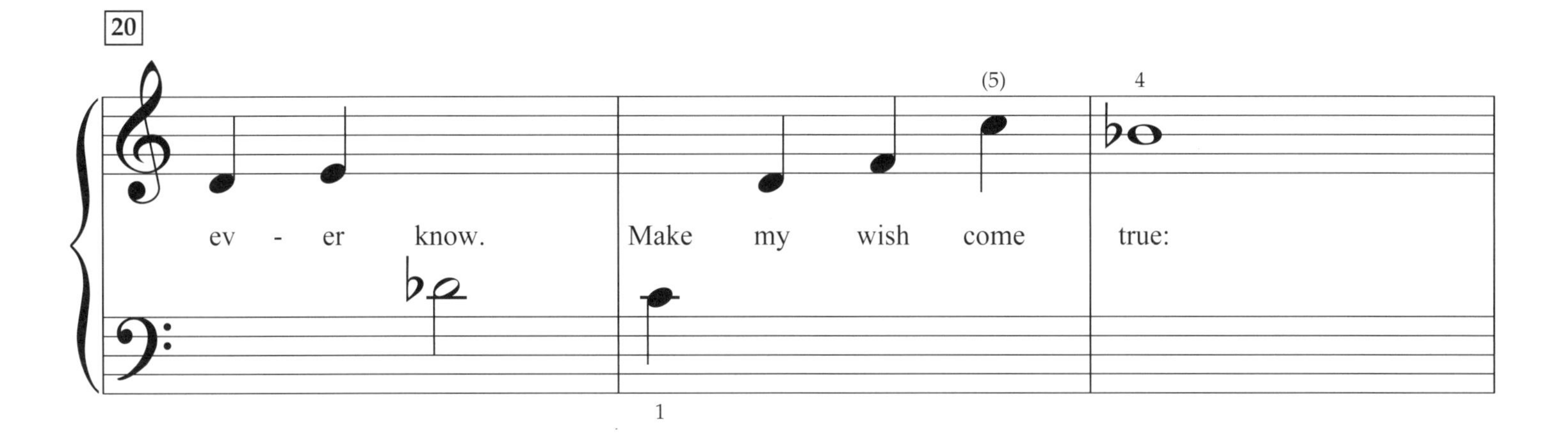
20
(5)
4
ev - er know.
Make my wish come
true:
1

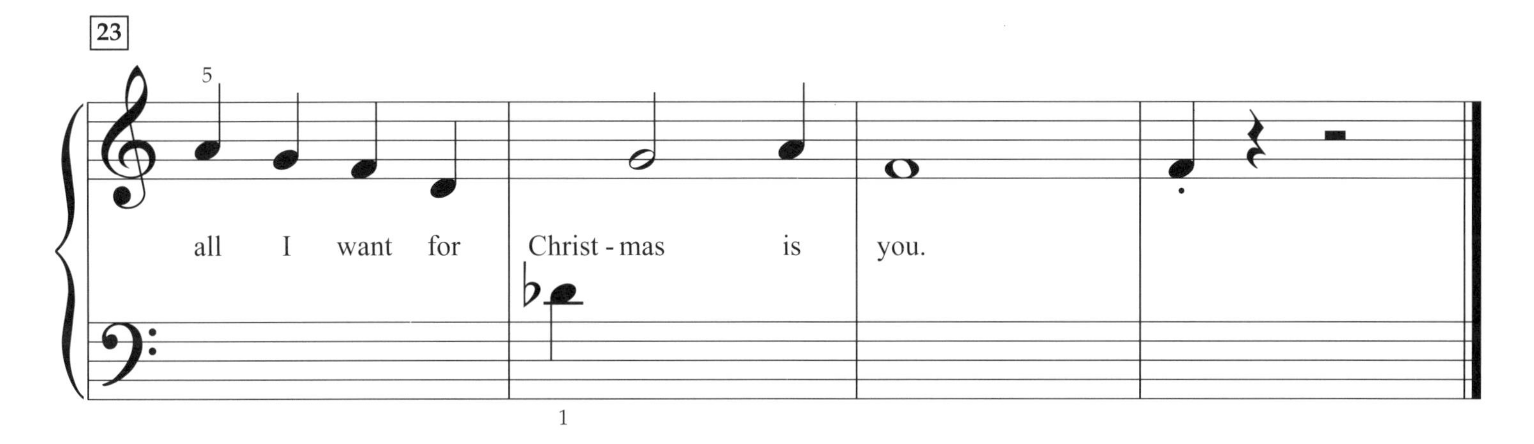
23
5
all I want for
Christ - mas is
you.
1

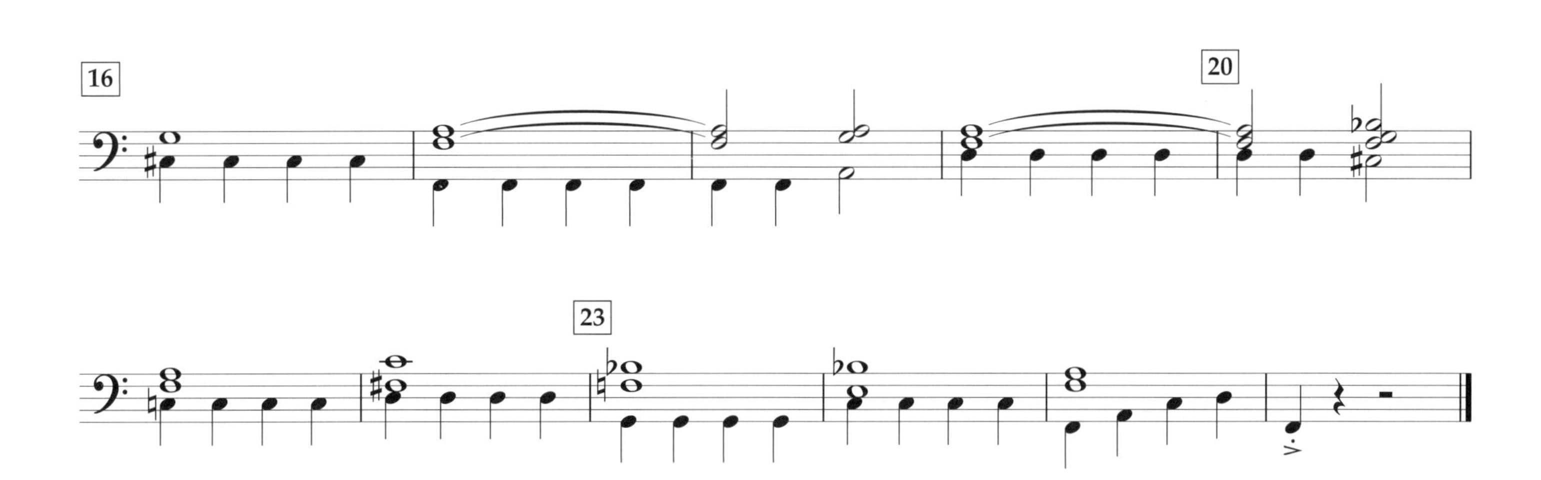
16
20
23

Believe
from Warner Bros. Pictures' THE POLAR EXPRESS

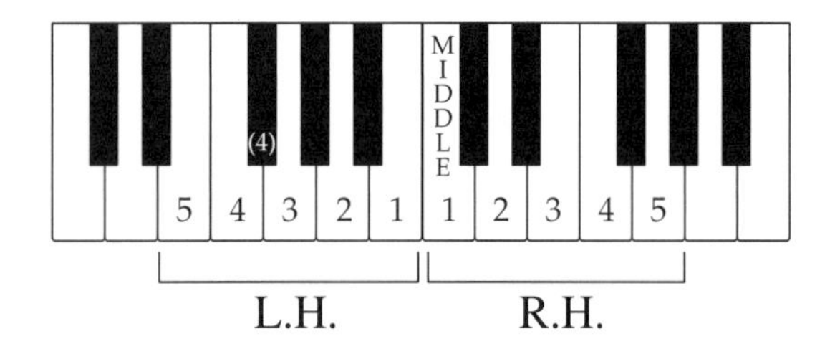

Words and Music by Glen Ballard
and Alan Silvestri

Moderately slow

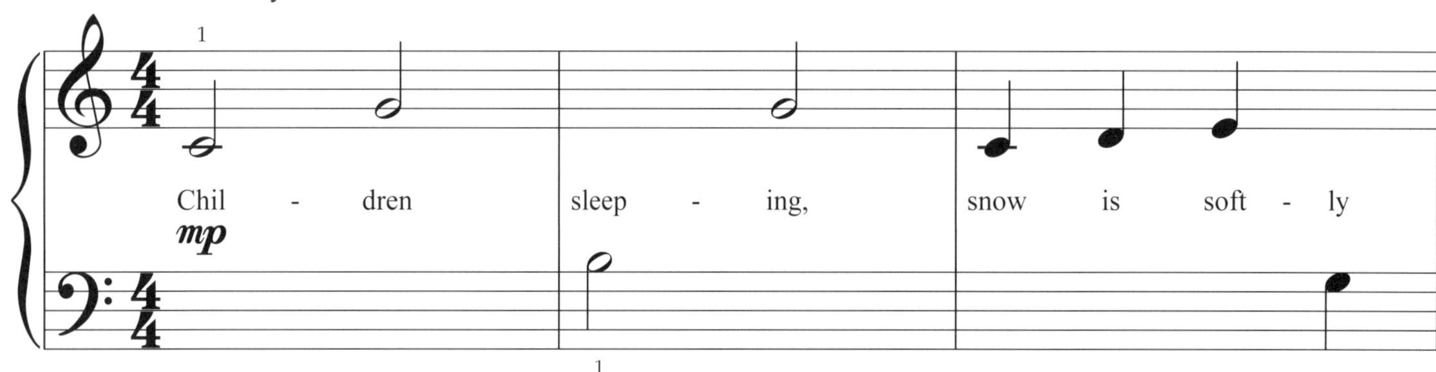

Duet Part (Student plays one octave higher than written.)

Moderately slow

8
dis - tance. We were dream - ers, not so long a -
3

12
go, but one by one, we all had to
(4)

16
grow up. When it seems the mag - ic slipped a - way, we
3

8
12
16

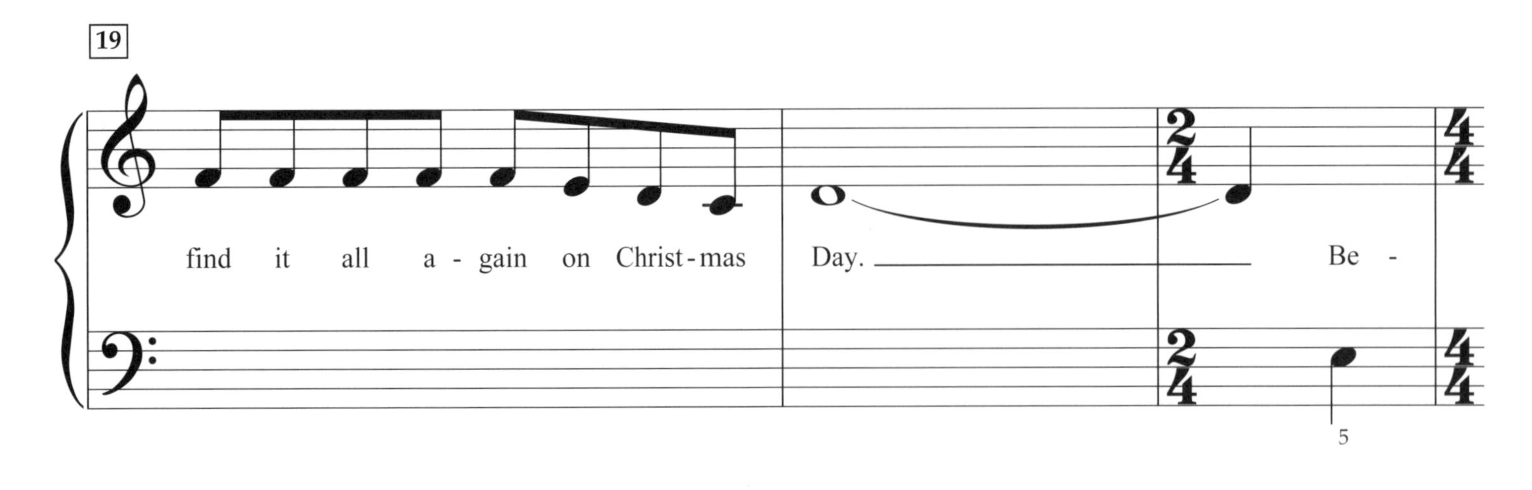
19
find it all a - gain on Christ - mas
Day.
Be -
5

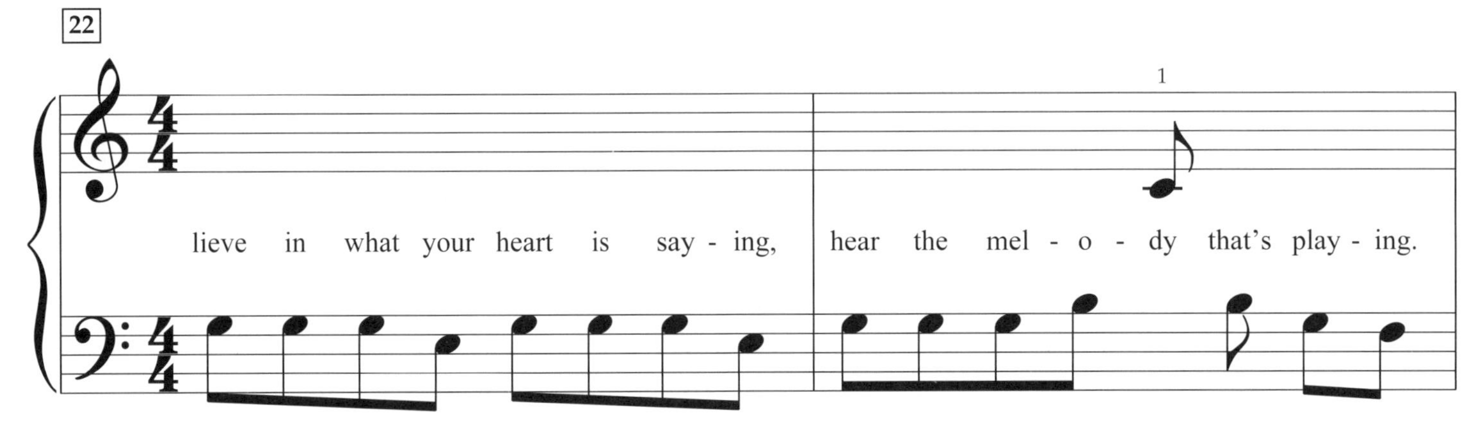
22
1
lieve in what your heart is say - ing,
hear the mel - o - dy that's play - ing.

24
There's no time to waste, there's so
much to cel - e - brate.
Be -
5

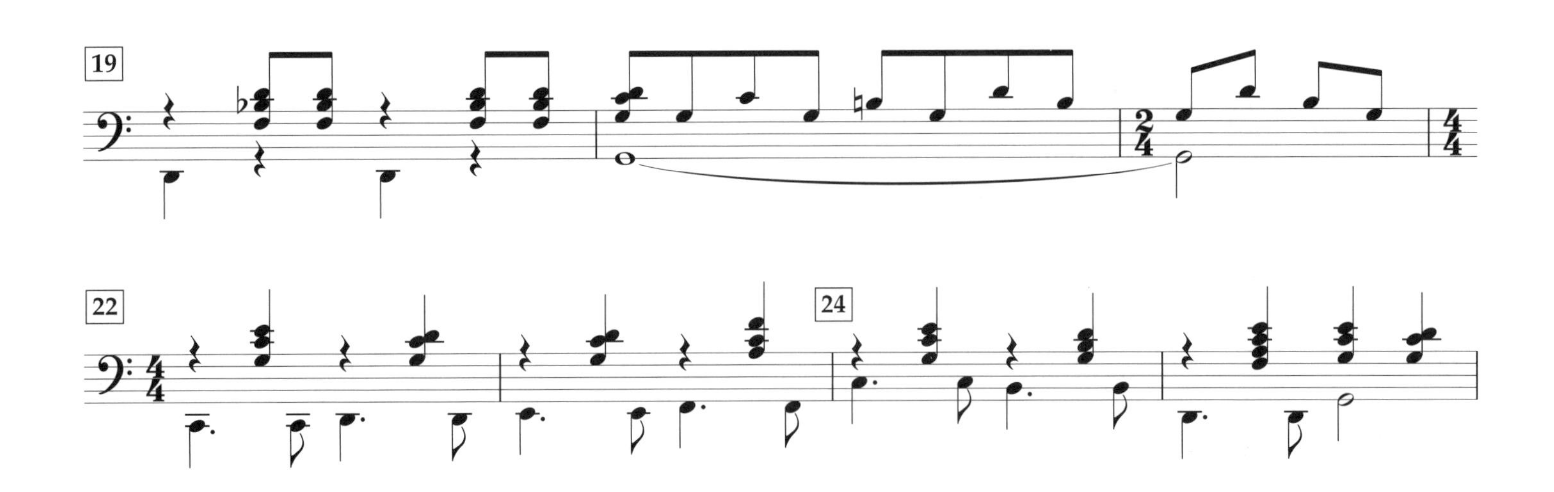
19
22
24

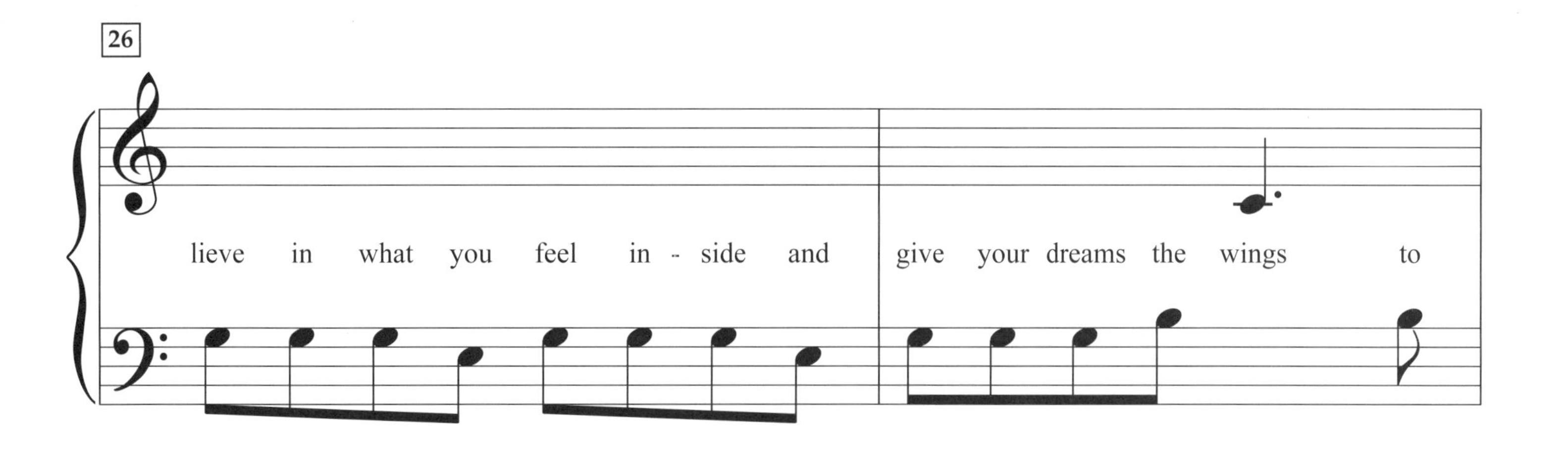
26
lieve in what you feel in - side and
give your dreams the wings to

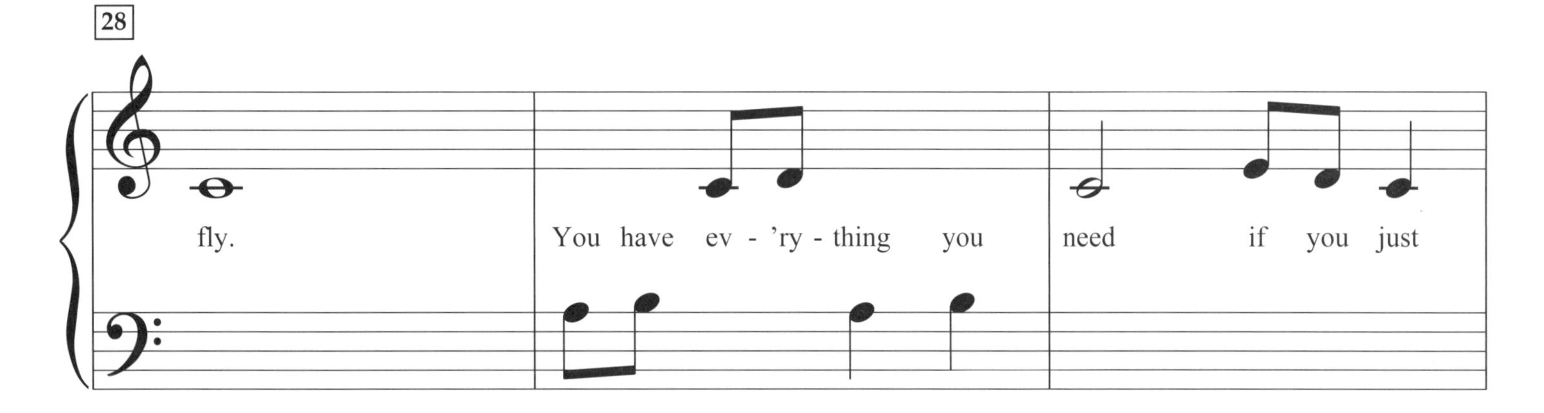
28
fly.
You have ev - 'ry - thing you
need if you just

31
be - lieve.
If you just
be - lieve.

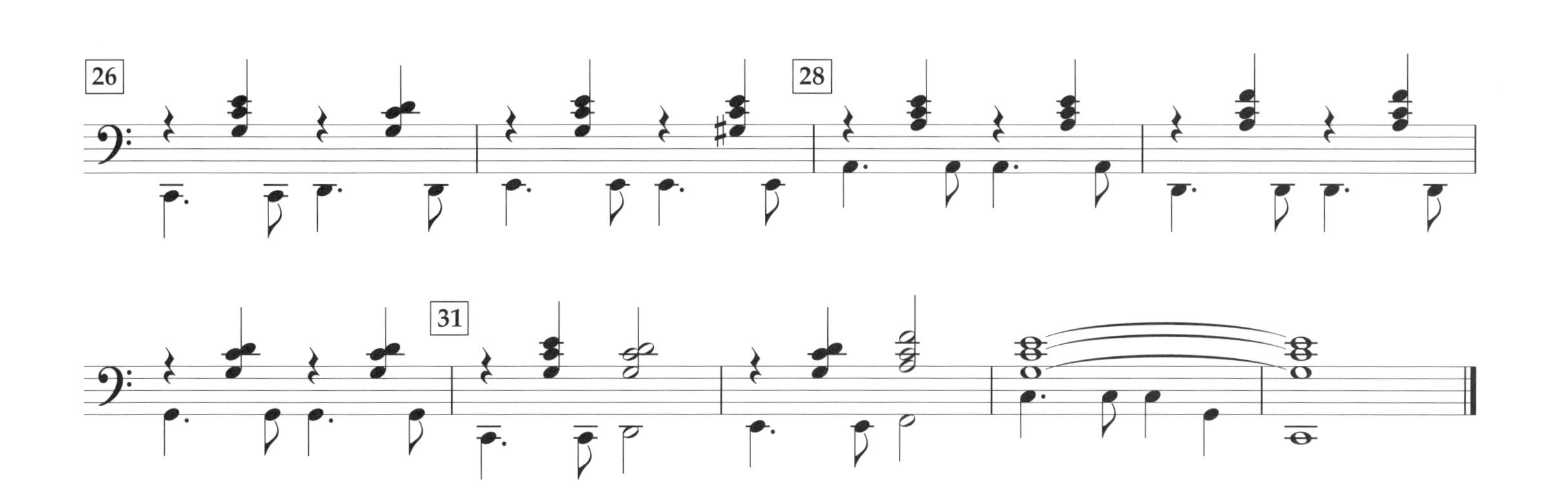
26
28
31

I Want a Hippopotamus for Christmas
(Hippo the Hero)

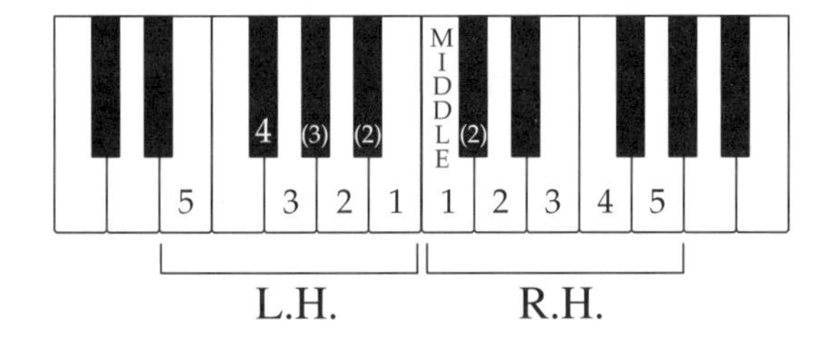

Words and Music by
John Rox

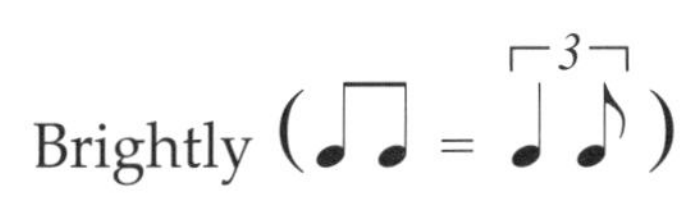

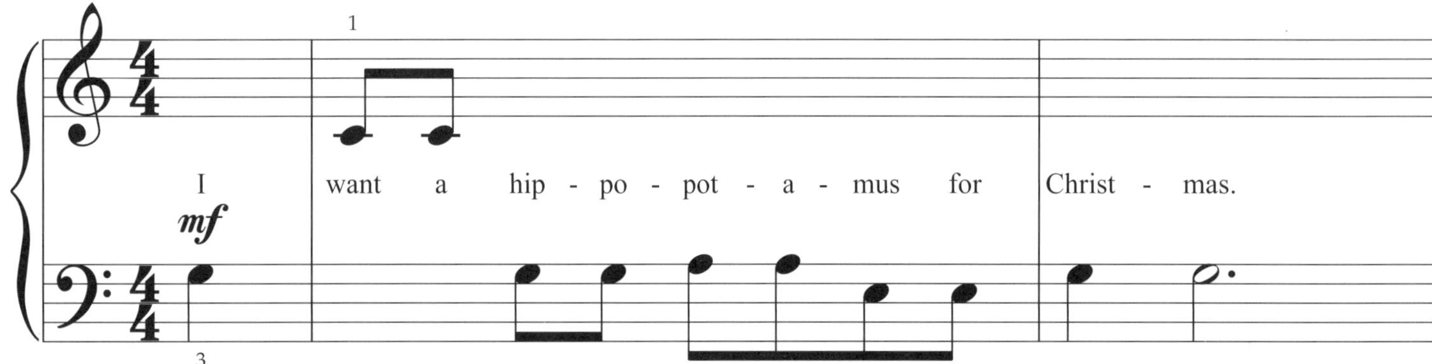

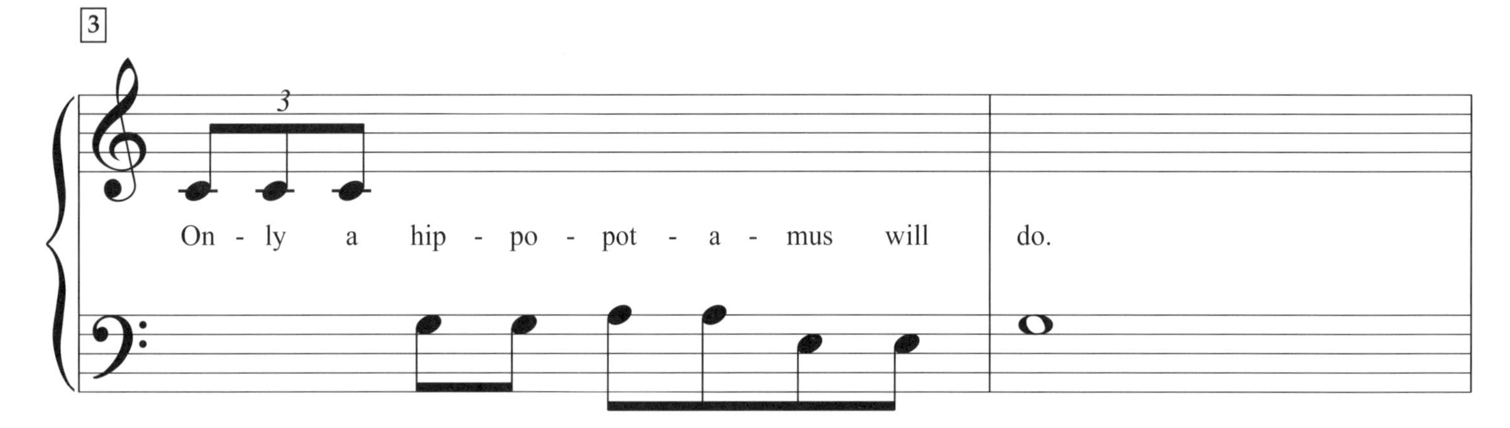

Duet Part (Student plays one octave higher than written.)

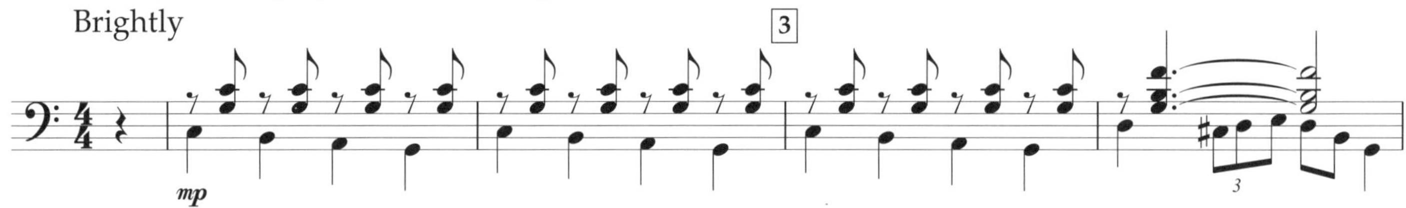

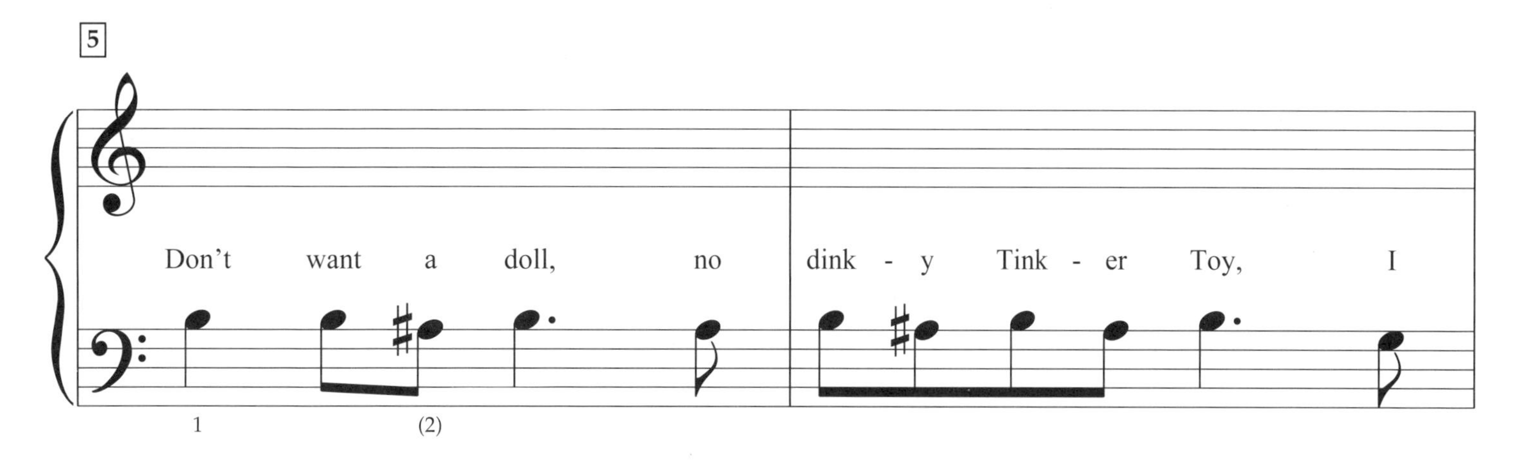
5
Don't want a doll, no dink - y Tink - er Toy, I
1
(2)

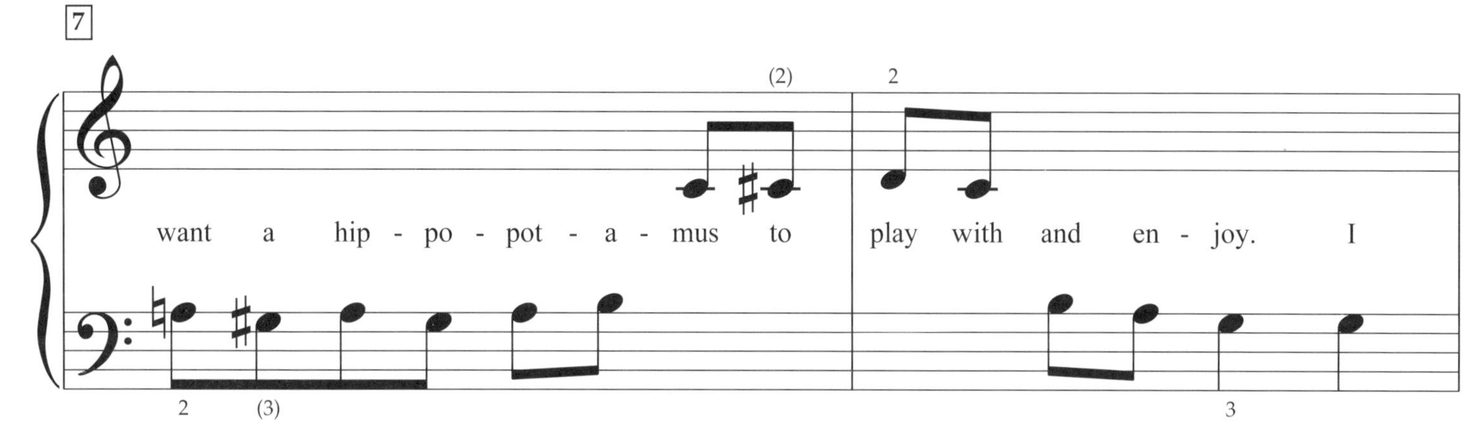
7
(2)
2
want a hip - po - pot - a - mus to play with and en - joy. I
2
(3)
3

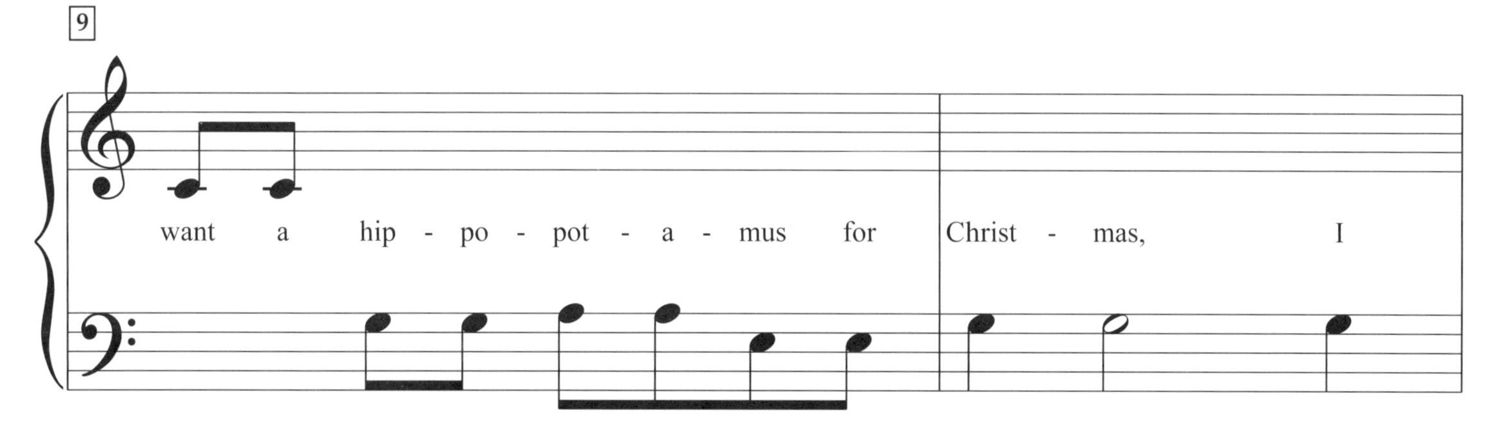
9
want a hip - po - pot - a - mus for Christ - mas, I

5
7
9

11
don't think San - ta Claus would mind, do
you? He

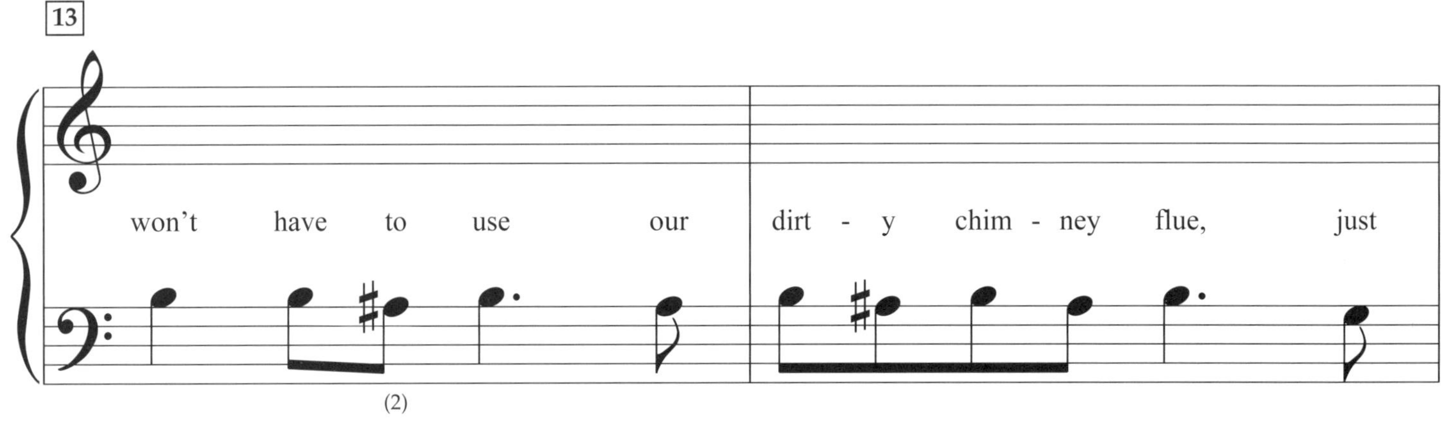
13
won't have to use our
dirt - y chim - ney flue, just

15
bring him through the front door, that's the
eas - y thing to do. I can

11
13
15

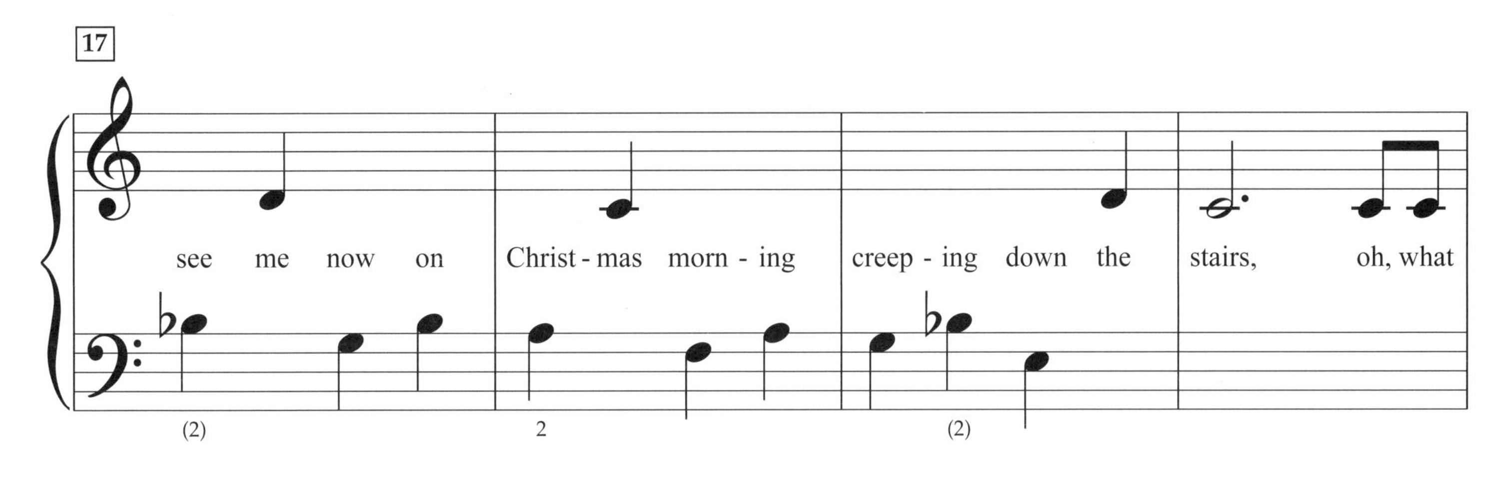
17
see me now on
Christ - mas morn - ing
creep - ing down the
stairs, oh, what
(2)
2
(2)

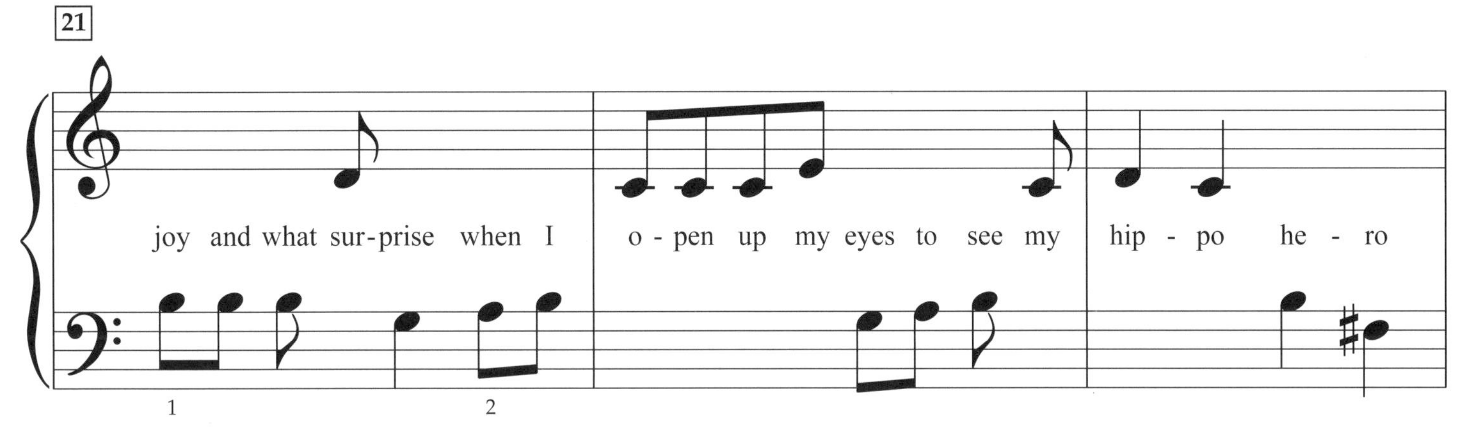
21
joy and what sur - prise when I
o - pen up my eyes to see my
hip - po he - ro
1
2

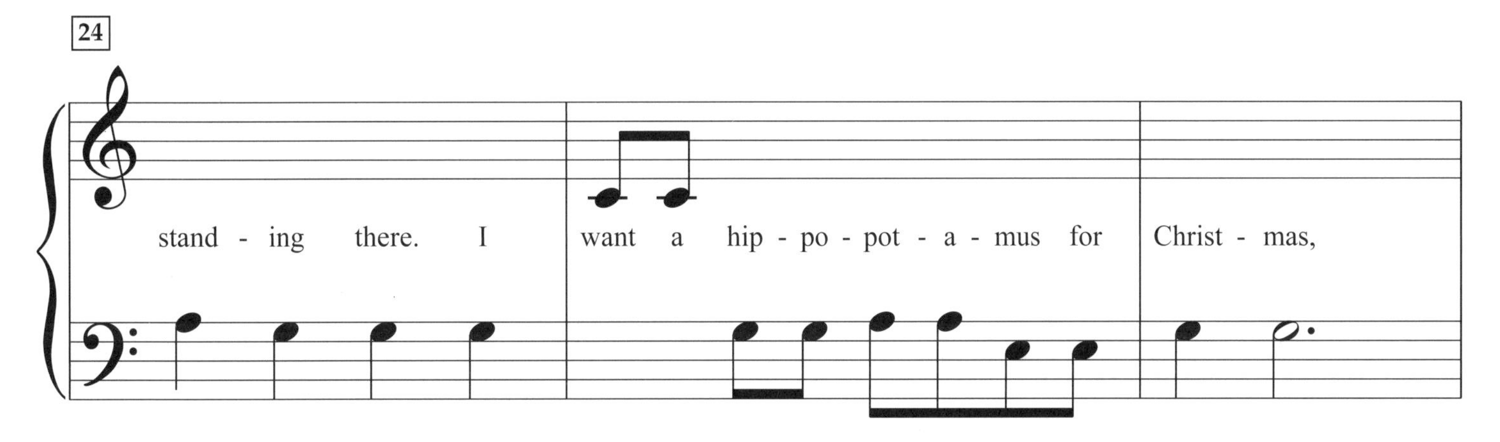
24
stand - ing there. I
want a hip - po - pot - a - mus for
Christ - mas,

17
21
24

27
3
on - ly a hip - po - pot - a - mus will
do.
No croc - o - diles or

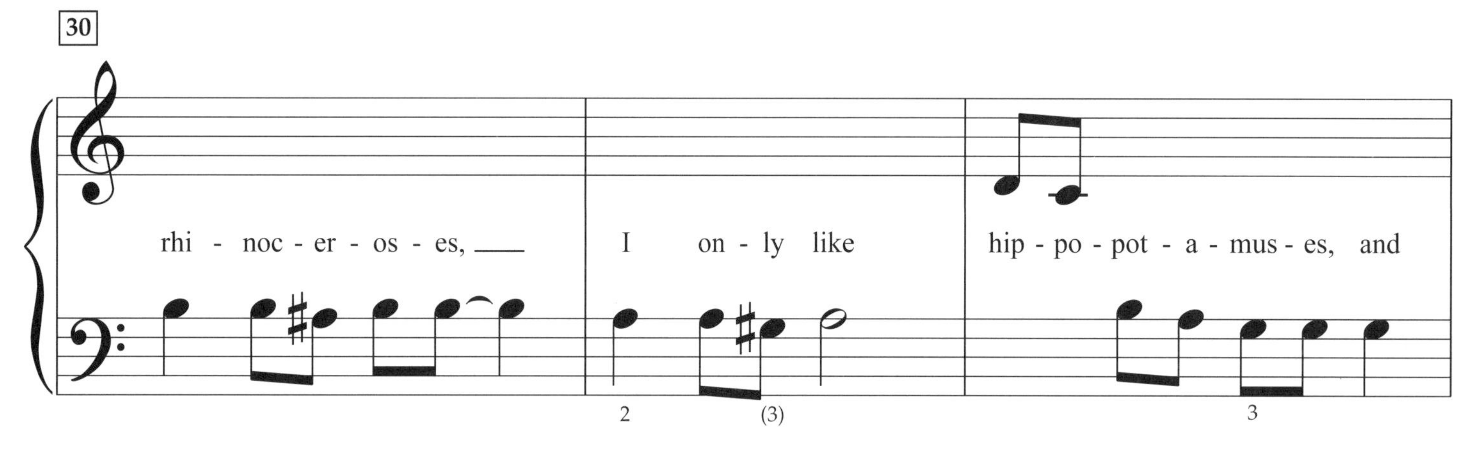
30
rhi - noc - er - os - es,
I on - ly like
hip - po - pot - a - mus - es, and
2
(3)
3

33
hip - po - pot - a - mus - es like me,
too.
(3)
(2)

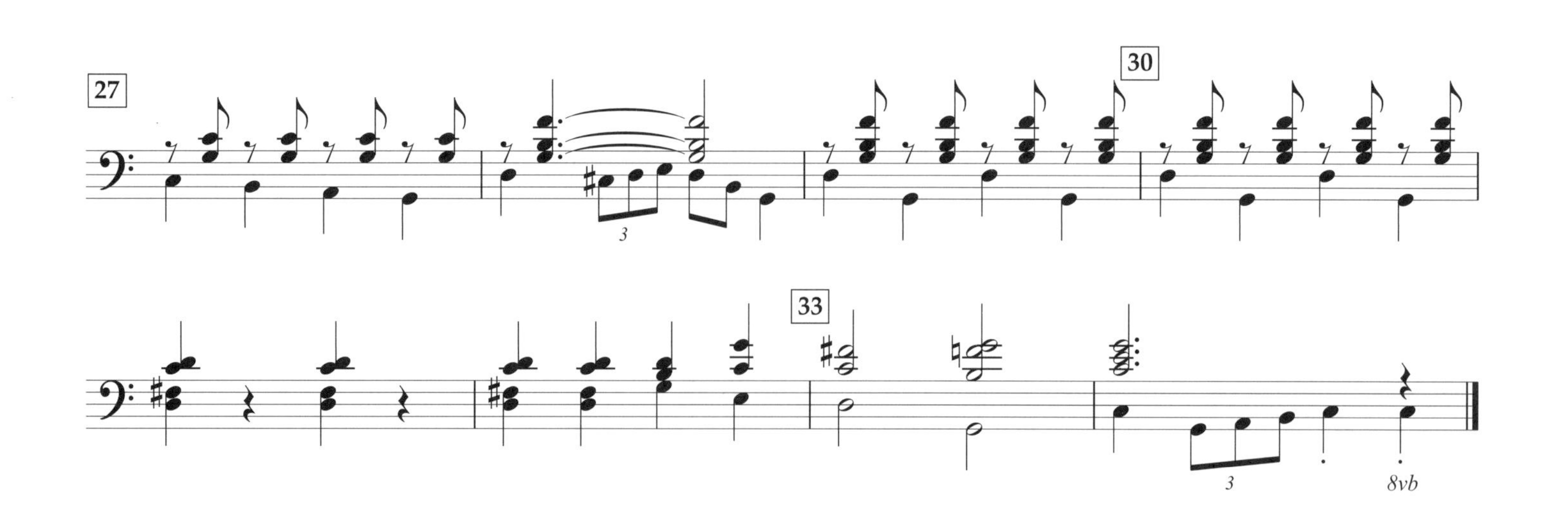
27
30
3
33
3
8vb

It's Beginning to Look Like Christmas

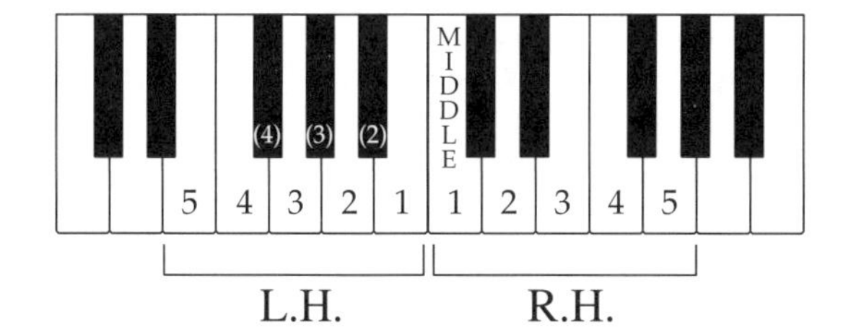

By Meredith Willson

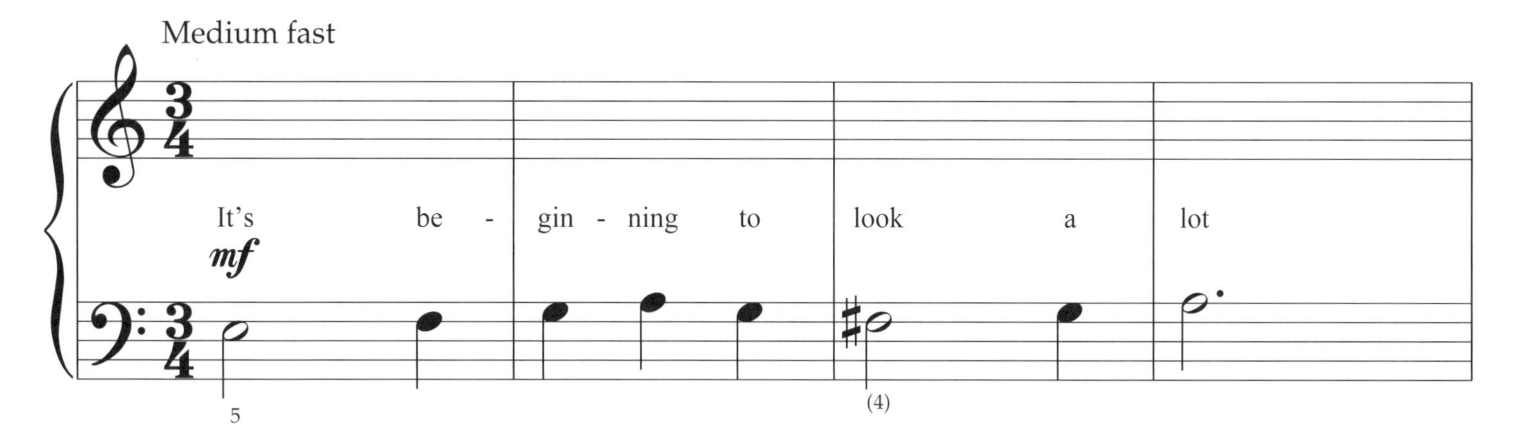

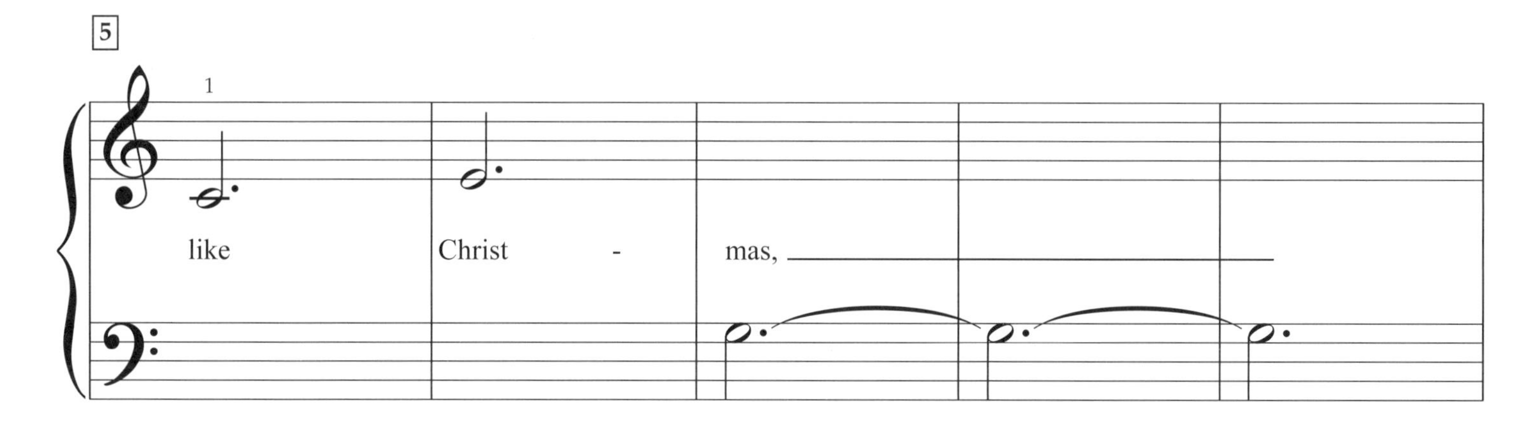

Duet Part (Student plays one octave higher than written.)

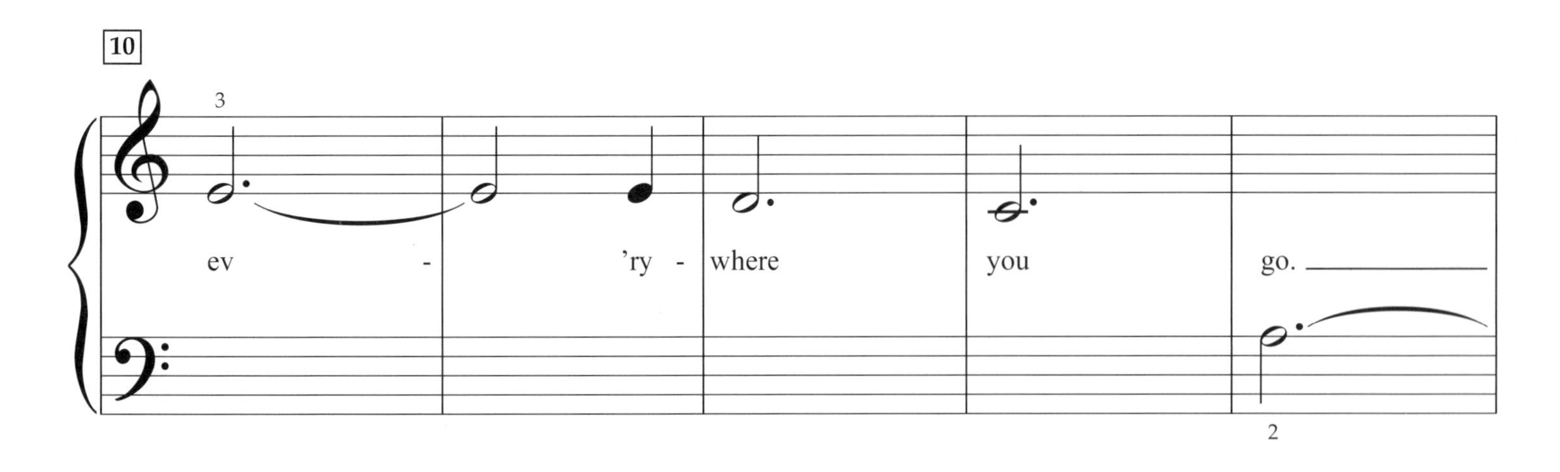
10
ev - 'ry - where you go.

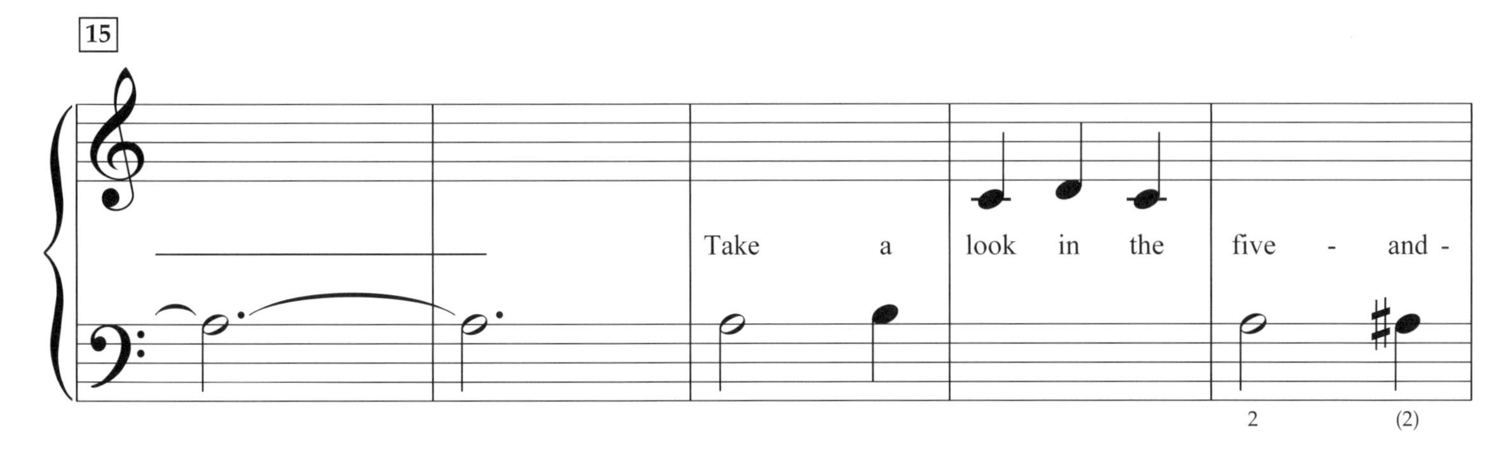
15
Take a look in the five - and -

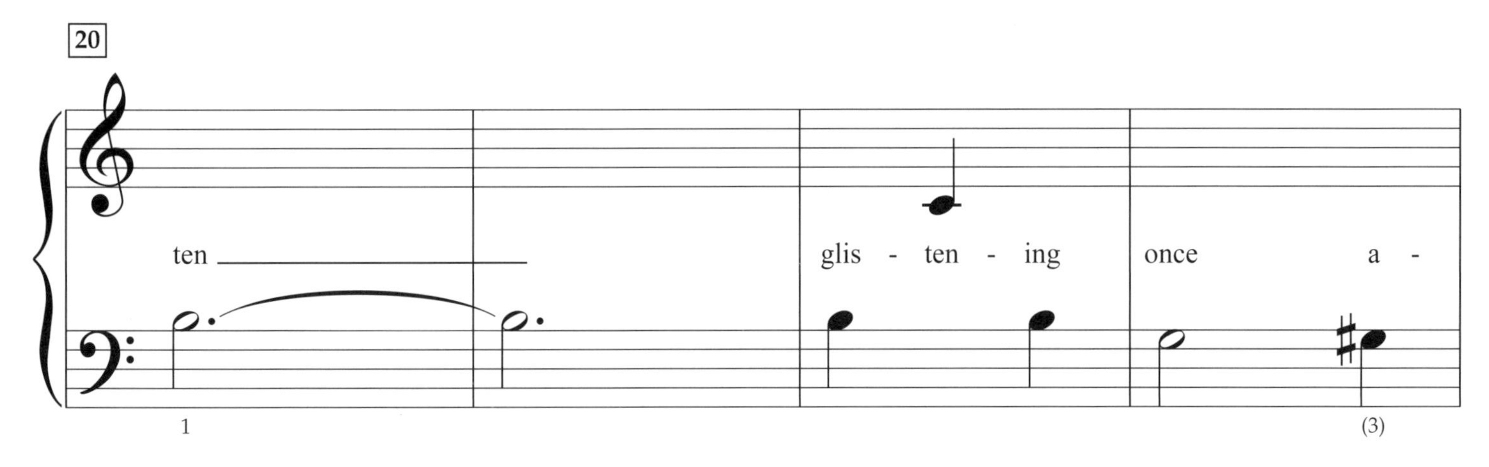
20
ten glis - ten - ing once a -

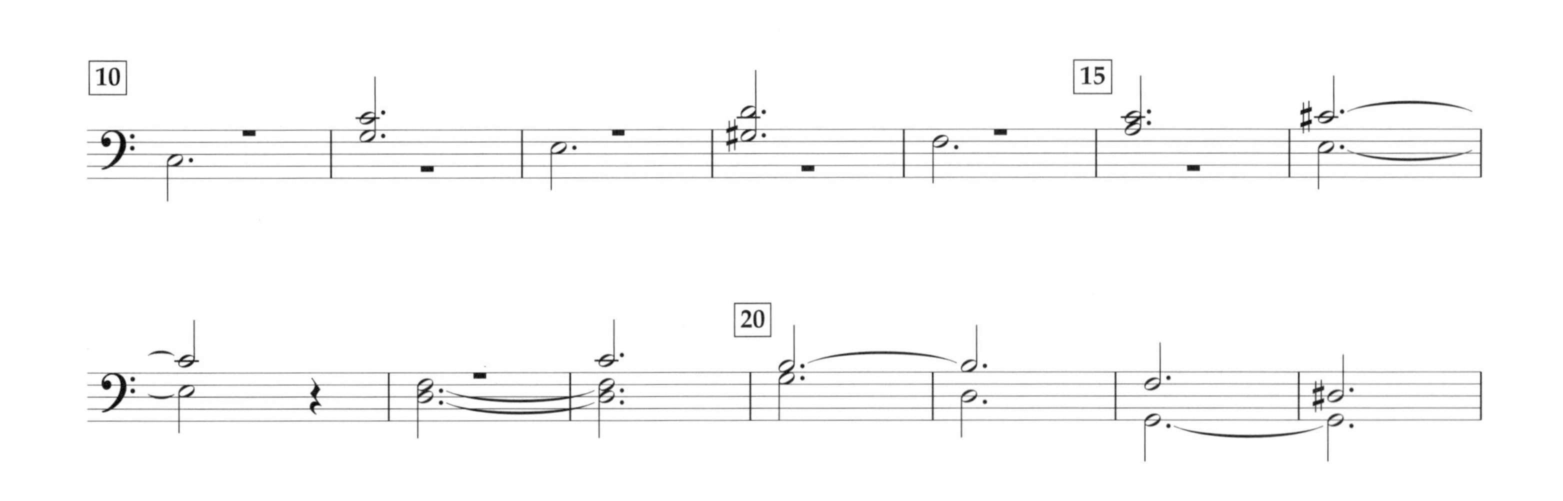
10
15
20

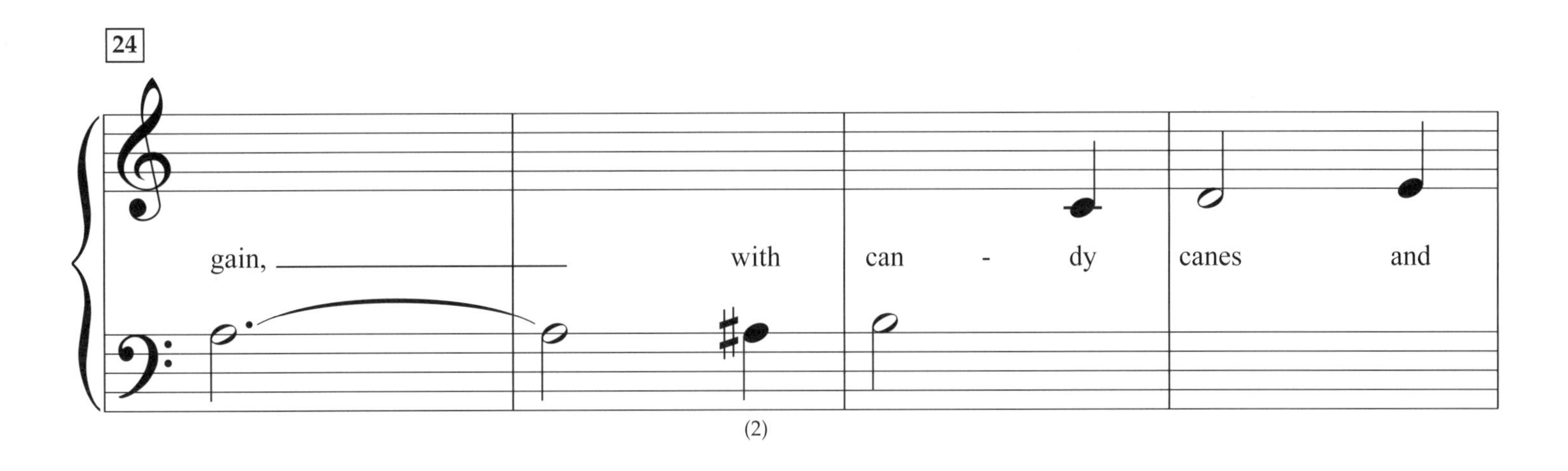
24
gain, with can - dy canes and
(2)

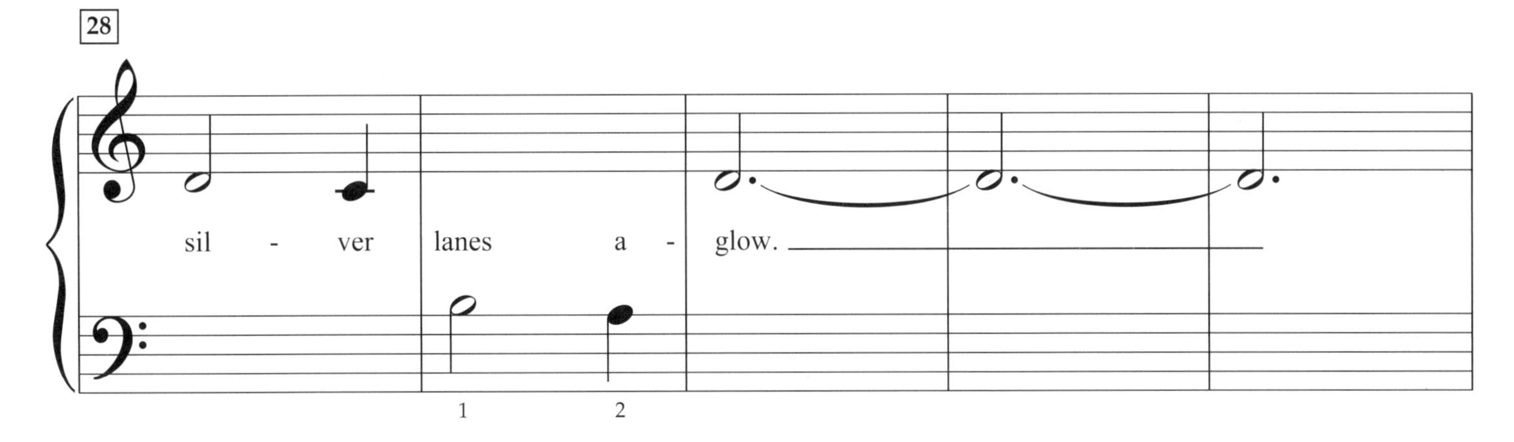
28
sil - ver lanes a - glow.
1 2

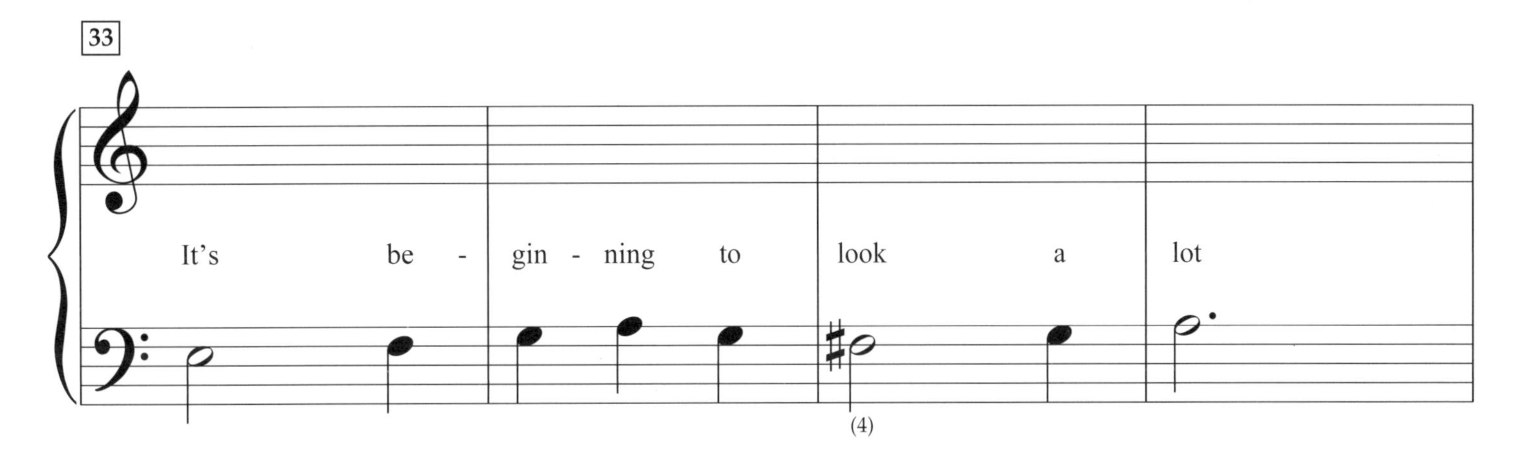
33
It's be - gin - ning to look a lot
(4)

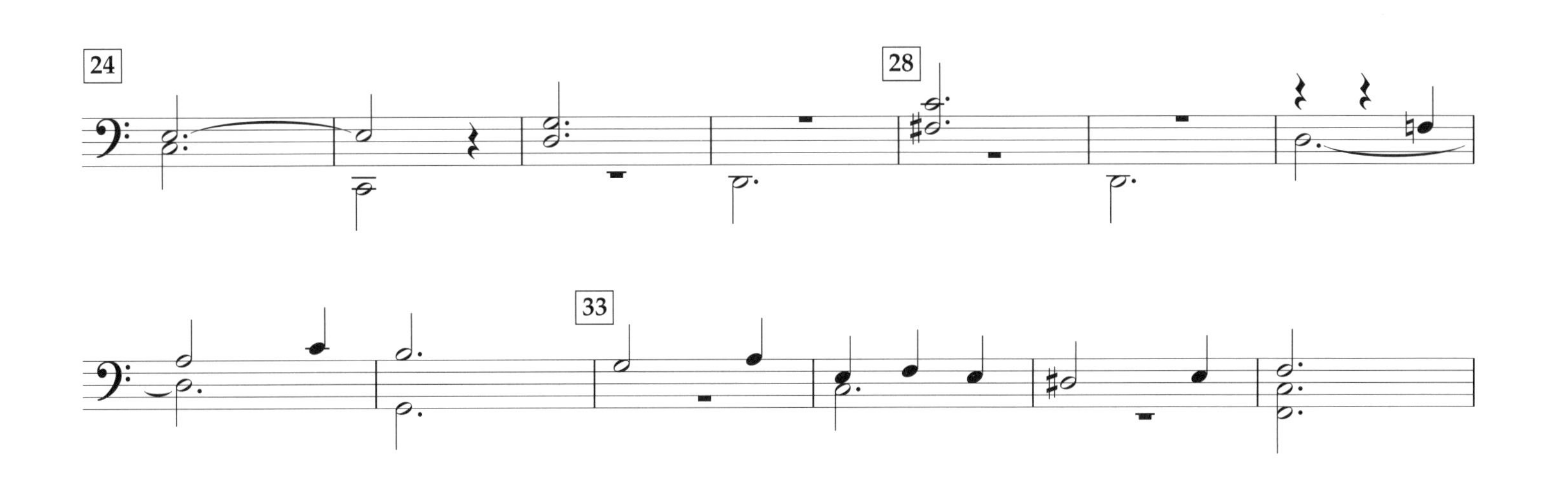
24
28
33

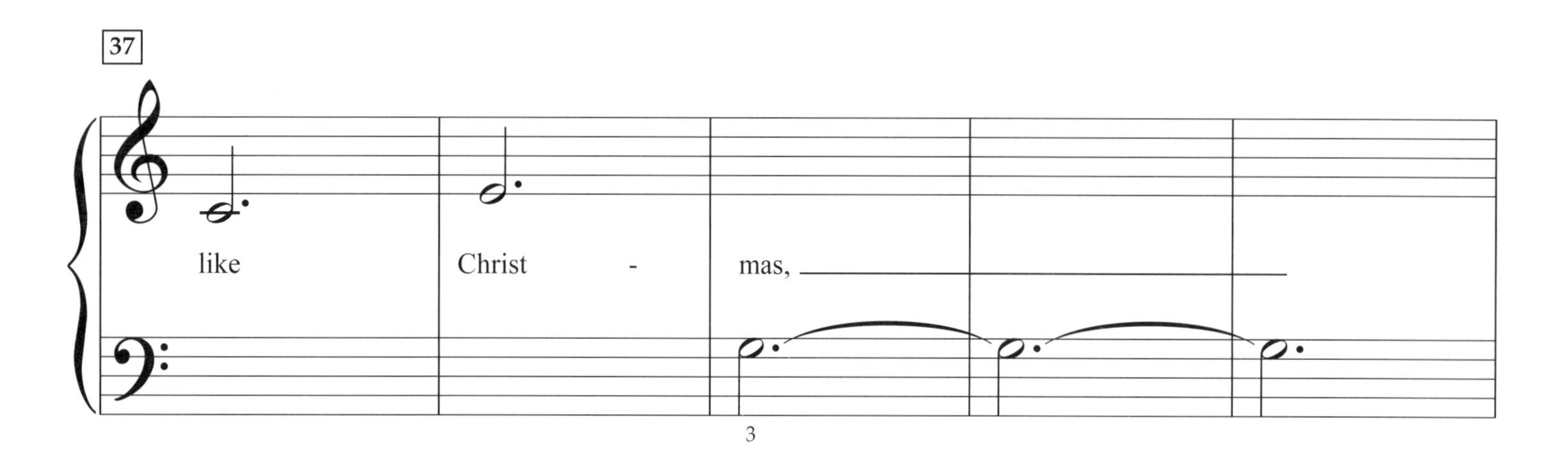
37
like Christ - mas,

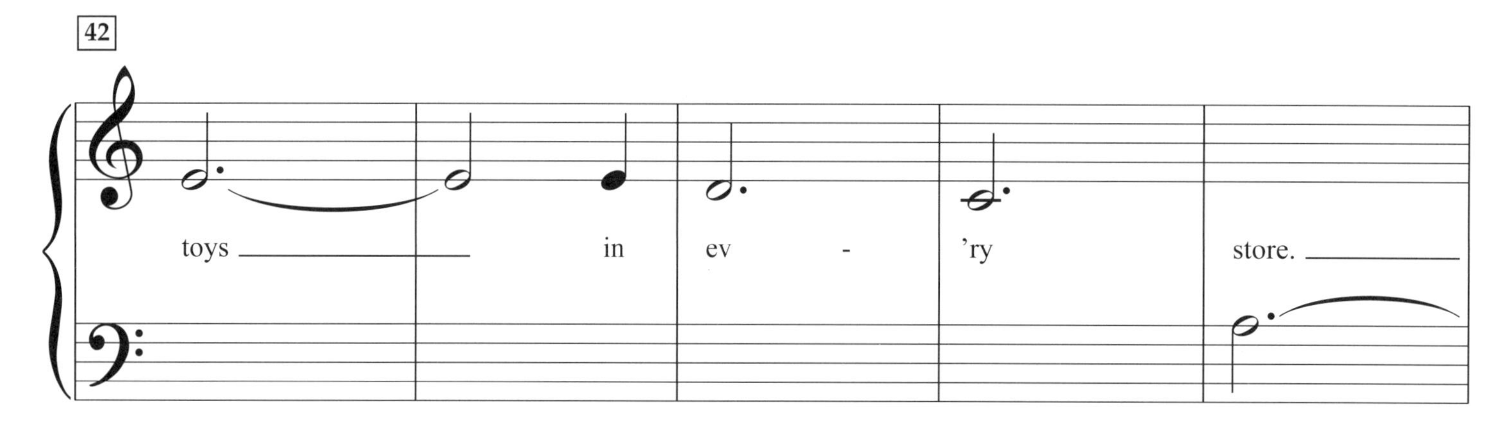
42
toys in ev - 'ry store.

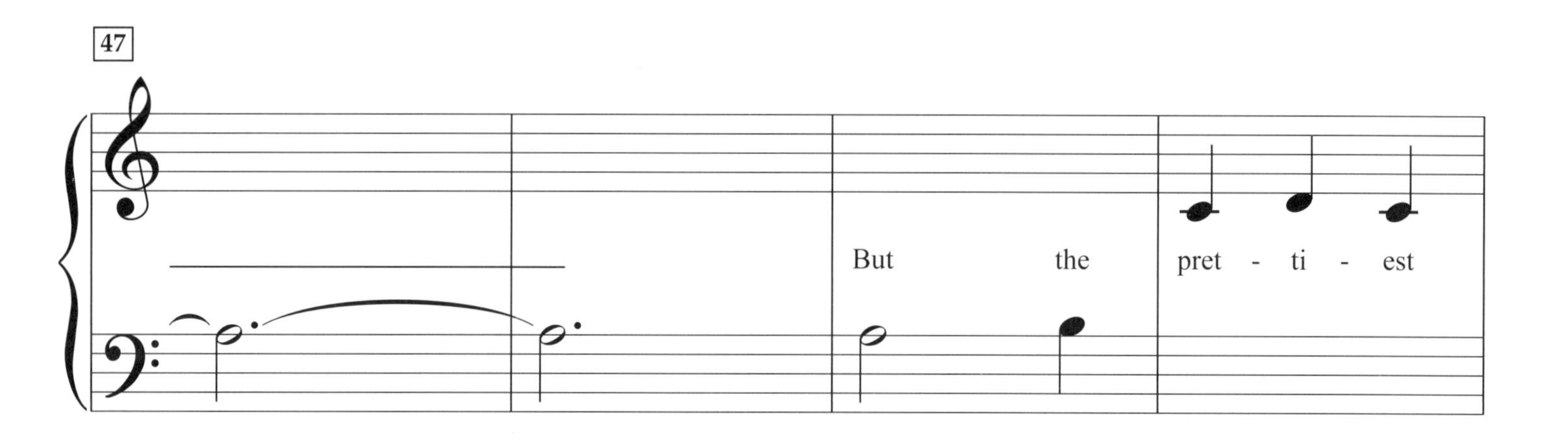
47
But the pret - ti - est

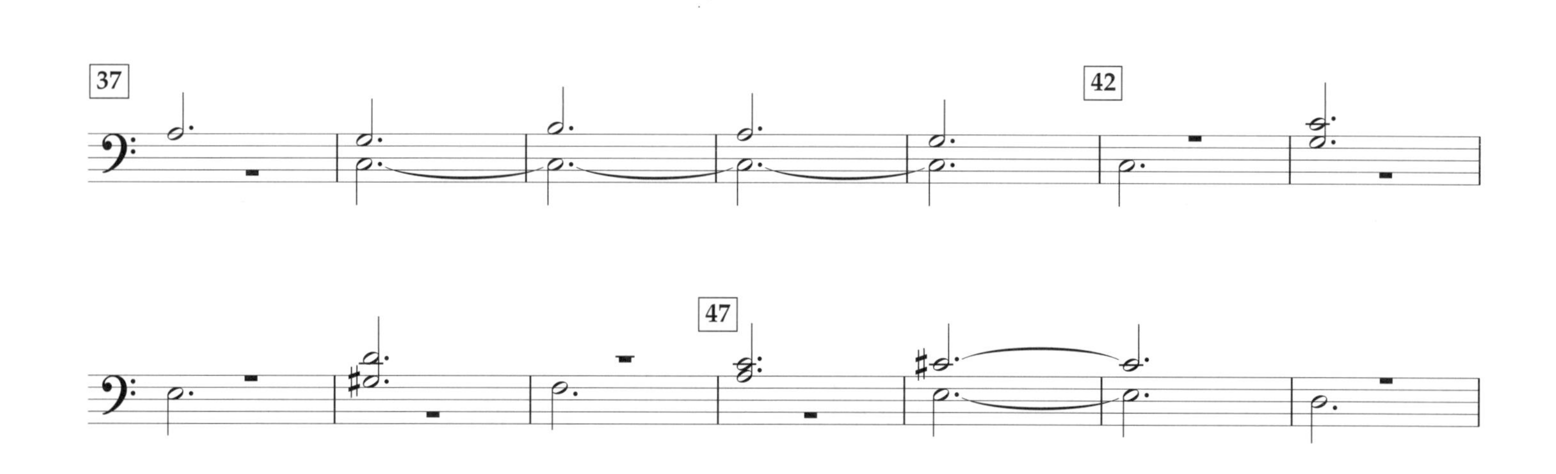
37
42
47

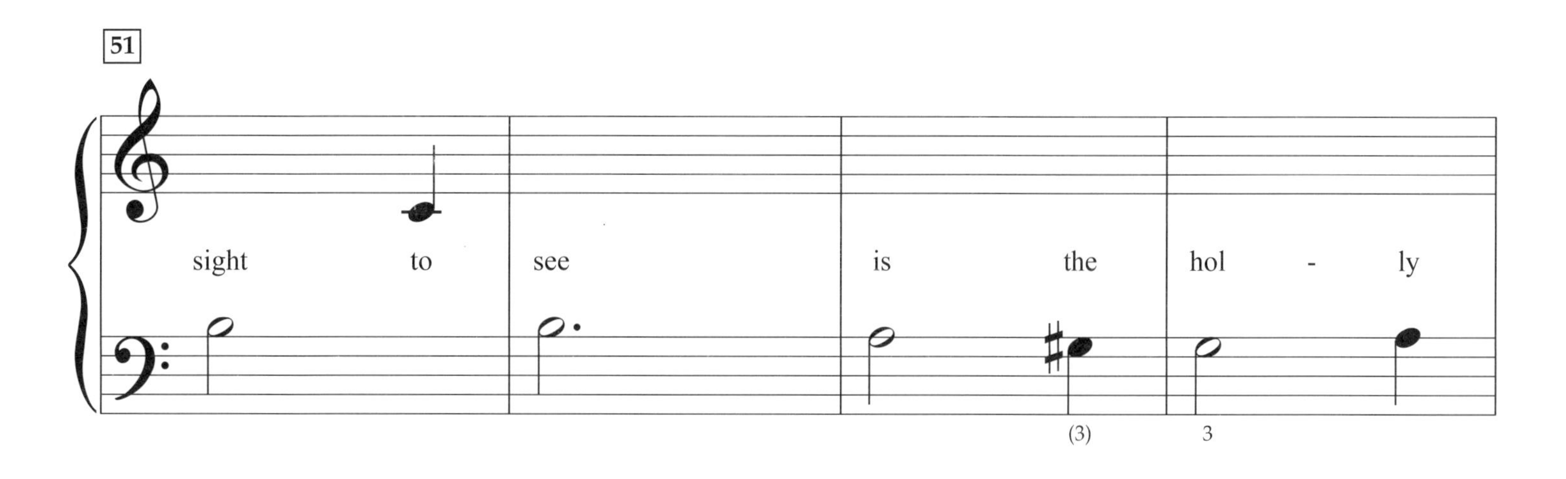
51
sight
to
see
is
the
hol
-
ly
(3)
3

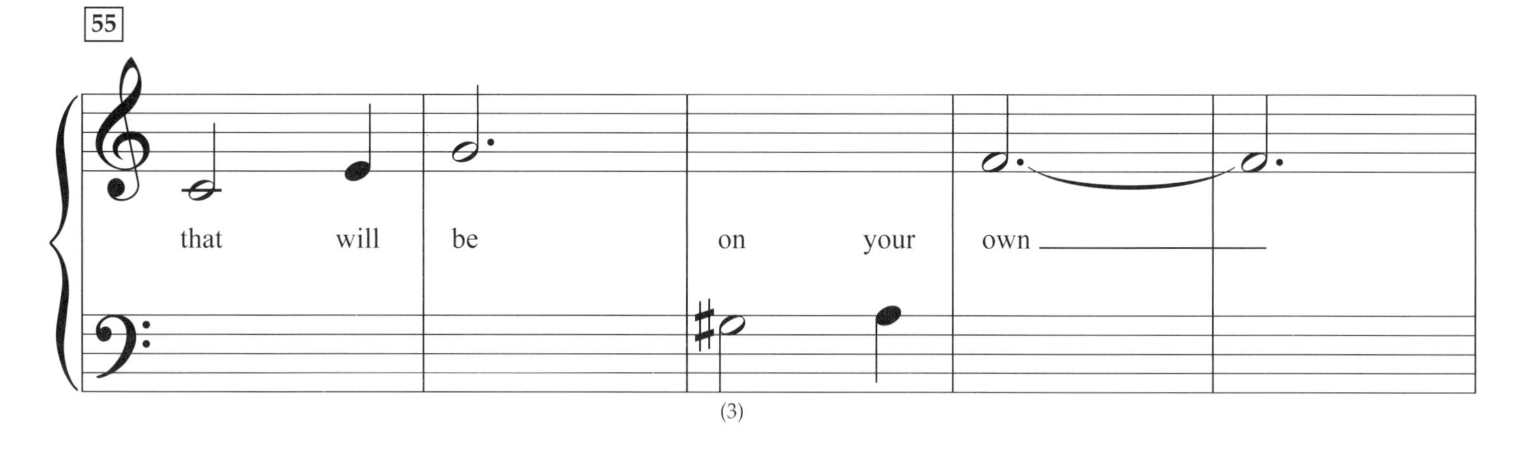
55
that
will
be
on
your
own
(3)

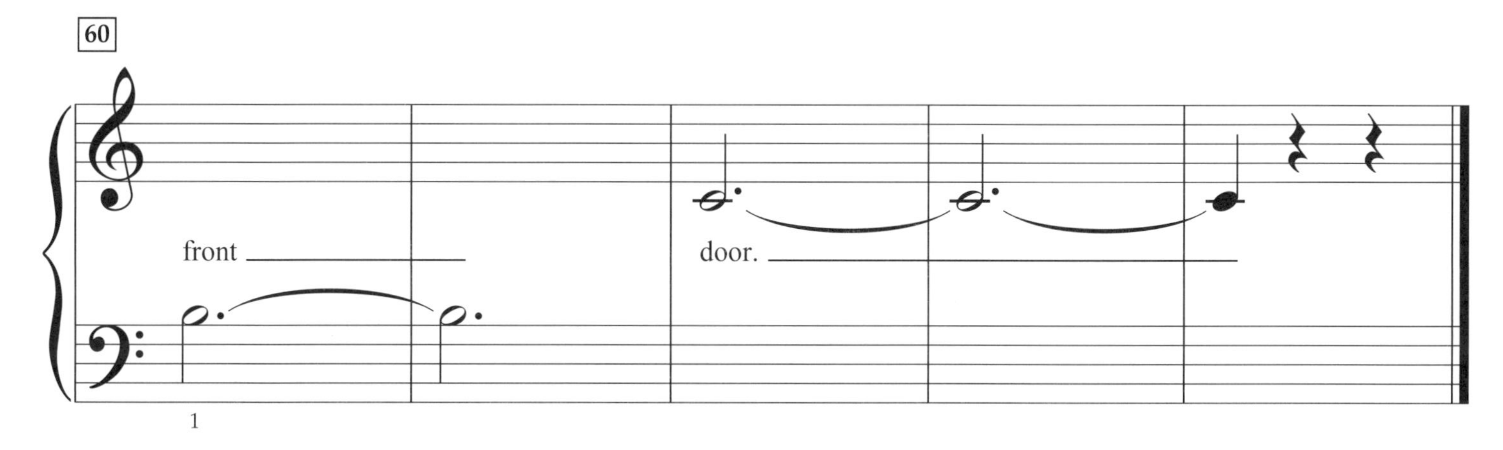
60
front
door.
1

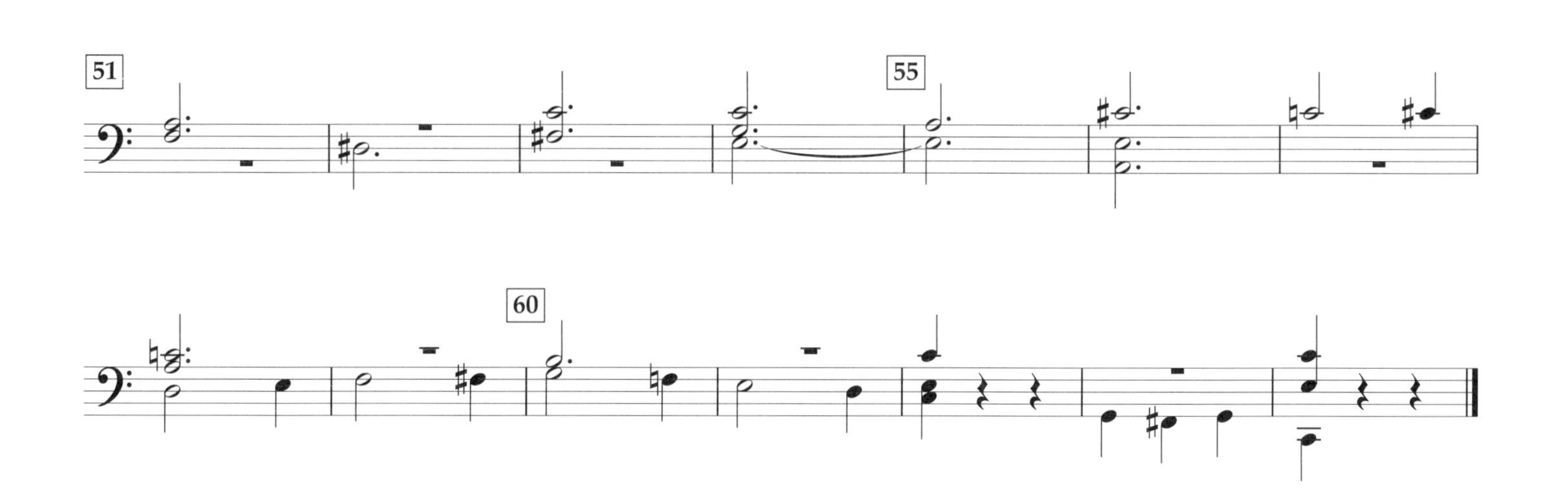
51
55
60

Santa Shark

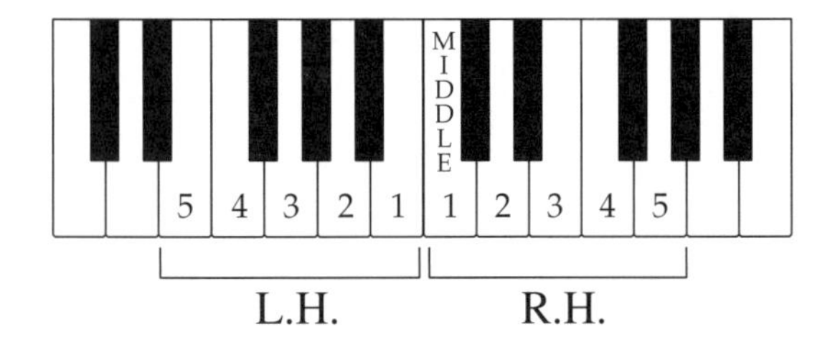

Traditional Nursery Rhyme
Arranged by Morghan Fortier,
James Jubinville, Troy McDonald,
Adam Sakiyama and Devin Thagard

With a bounce

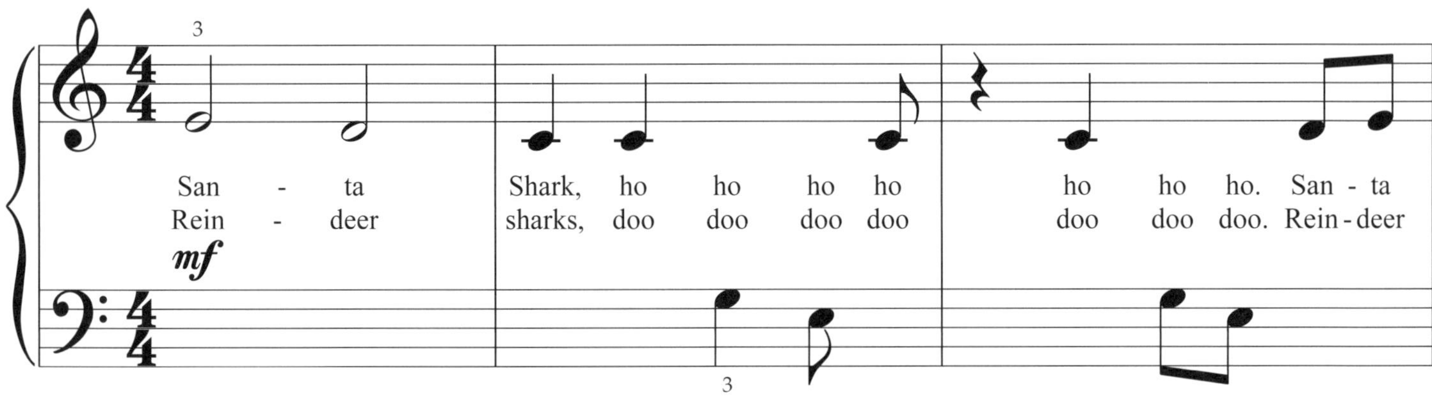

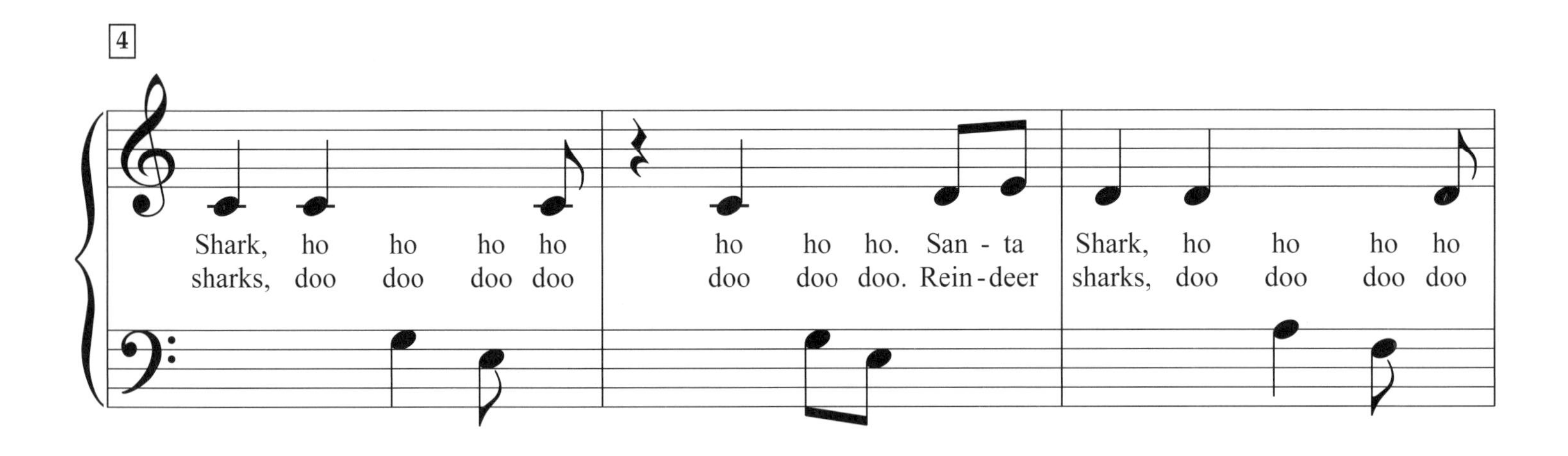

Duet Part (Student plays one octave higher than written.)

With a bounce

7
ho ho ho. San - ta Shark.
doo doo doo. Rein-deer sharks.
3
Elf sharks, doo doo doo doo
11
doo doo doo. Elf sharks, doo doo doo doo doo doo doo. Elf
14
sharks, doo doo doo doo doo doo doo. Elf sharks.
7
11
14

17
Mak - ing toys, doo doo doo doo doo doo doo. Mak - ing
San - ta Shark, ho ho ho ho ho ho ho. San - ta
20
toys, doo doo doo doo doo doo doo. Mak - ing toys, doo doo doo doo
Shark, ho ho ho ho ho ho ho. San - ta Shark, ho ho ho ho
23
1.
2.
doo doo doo. Mak - ing toys.
ho ho ho. San - ta Shark. It's Christ - mas!
17
20
23
1.
2.

Rudolph the Red-Nosed Reindeer

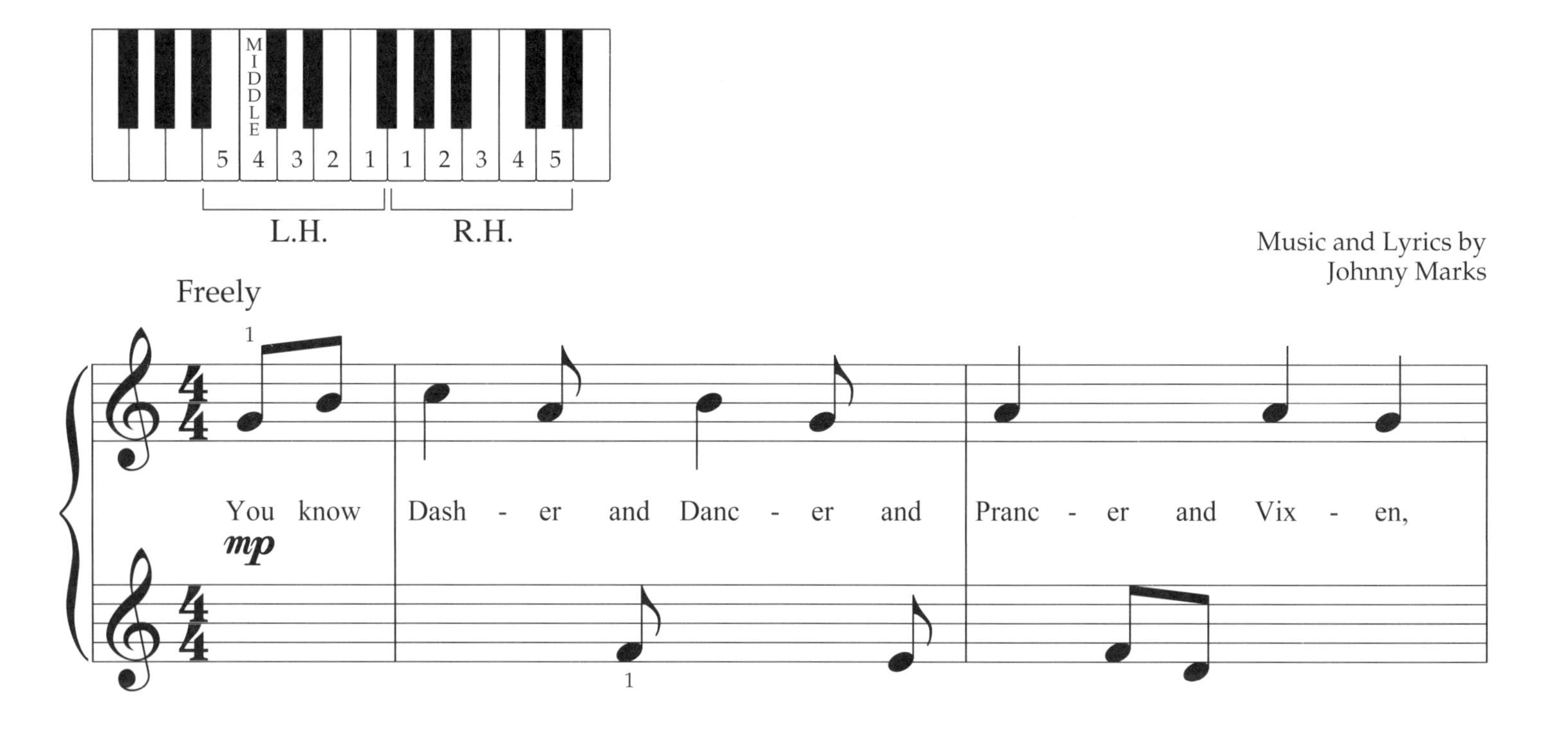

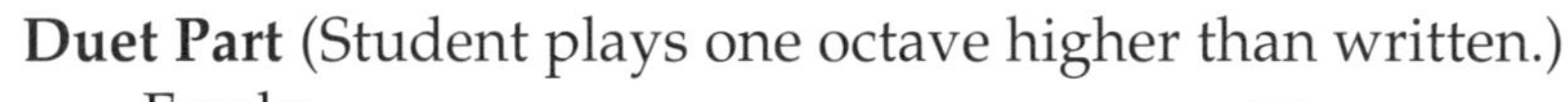
Duet Part (Student plays one octave higher than written.)

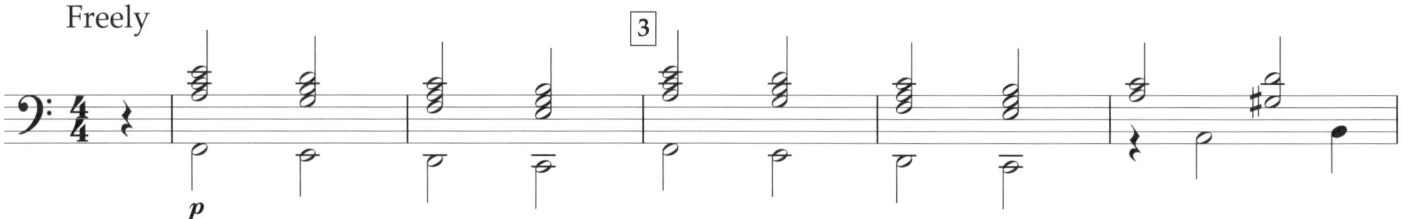

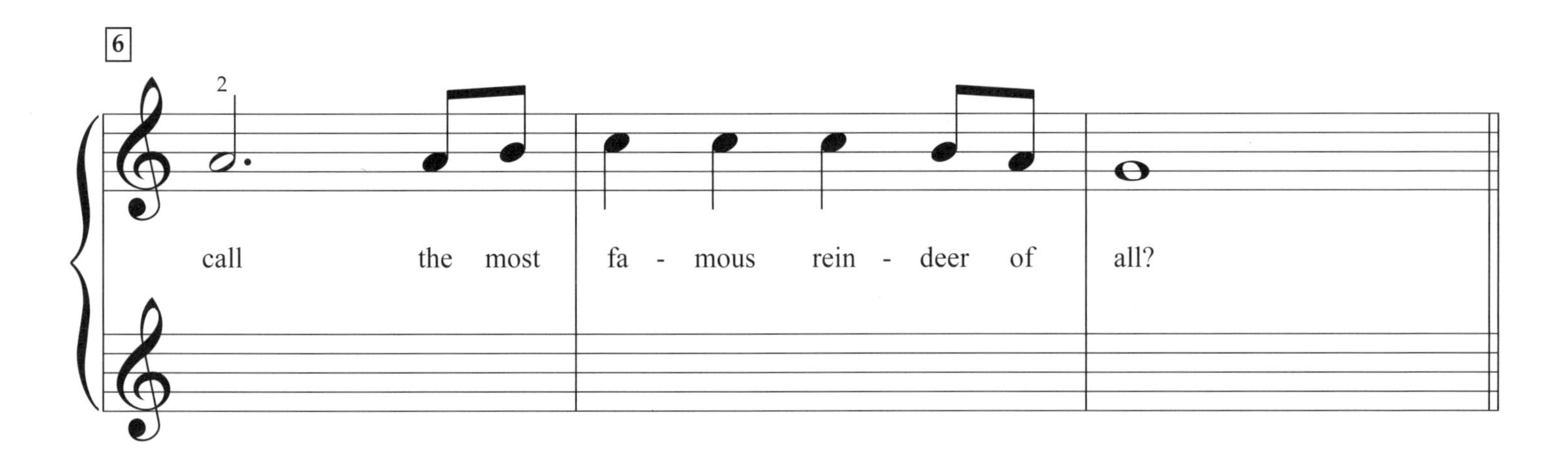
6
2
call the most fa - mous rein - deer of all?

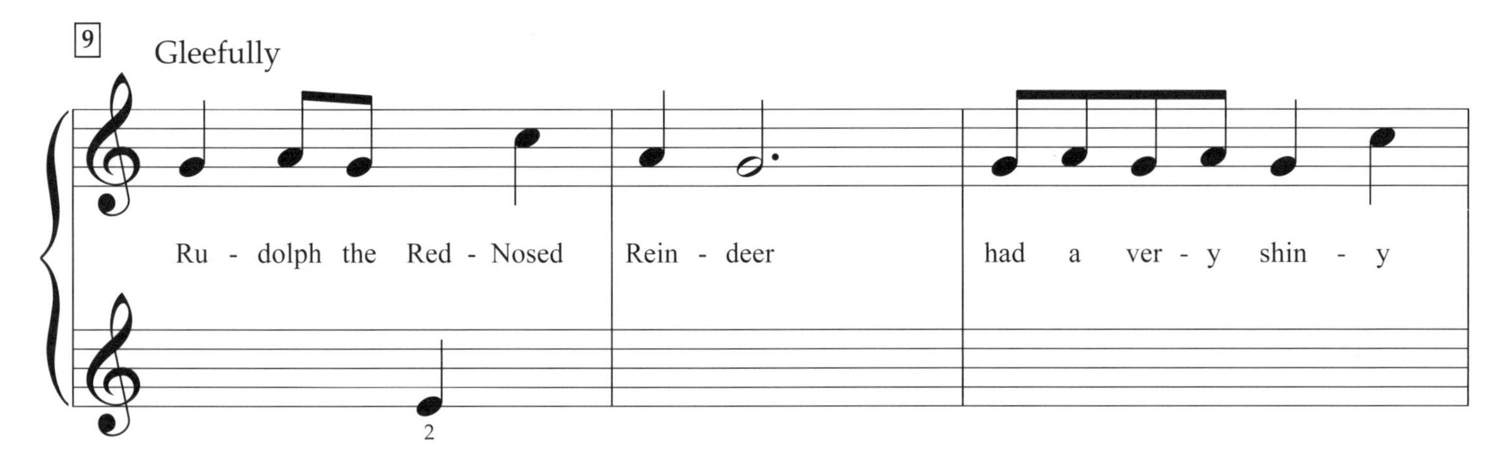
9
Gleefully
Ru - dolph the Red - Nosed Rein - deer had a ver - y shin - y
2

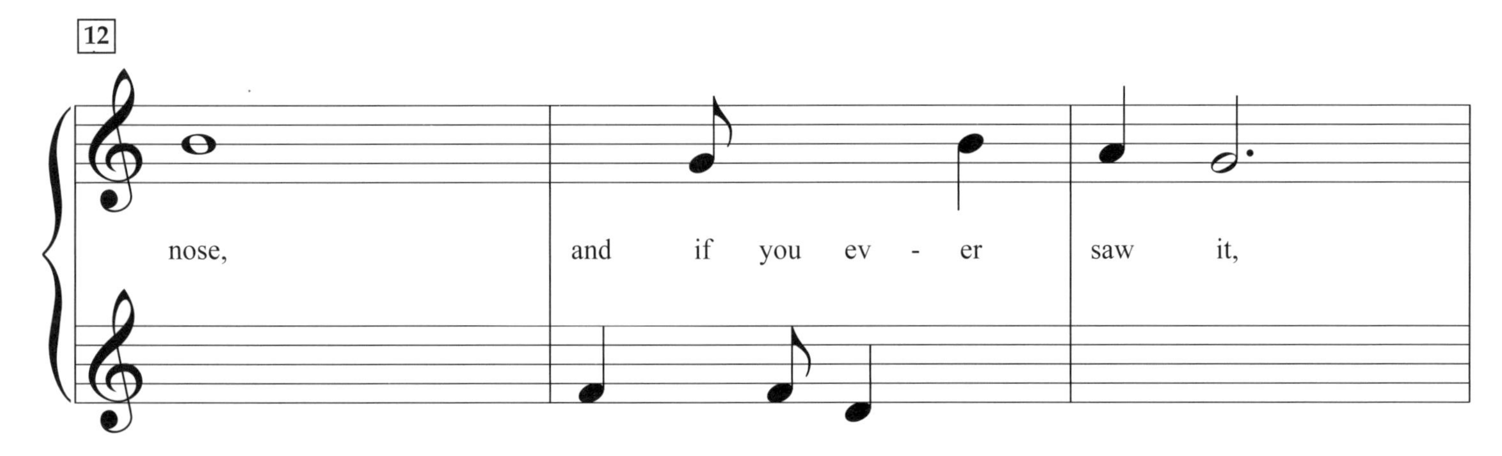
12
nose, and if you ev - er saw it,

Gleefully
6
9
mp
12

15
you would e - ven say it
glows.
All of the oth - er

18
rein - deer
used to laugh and call him
names.

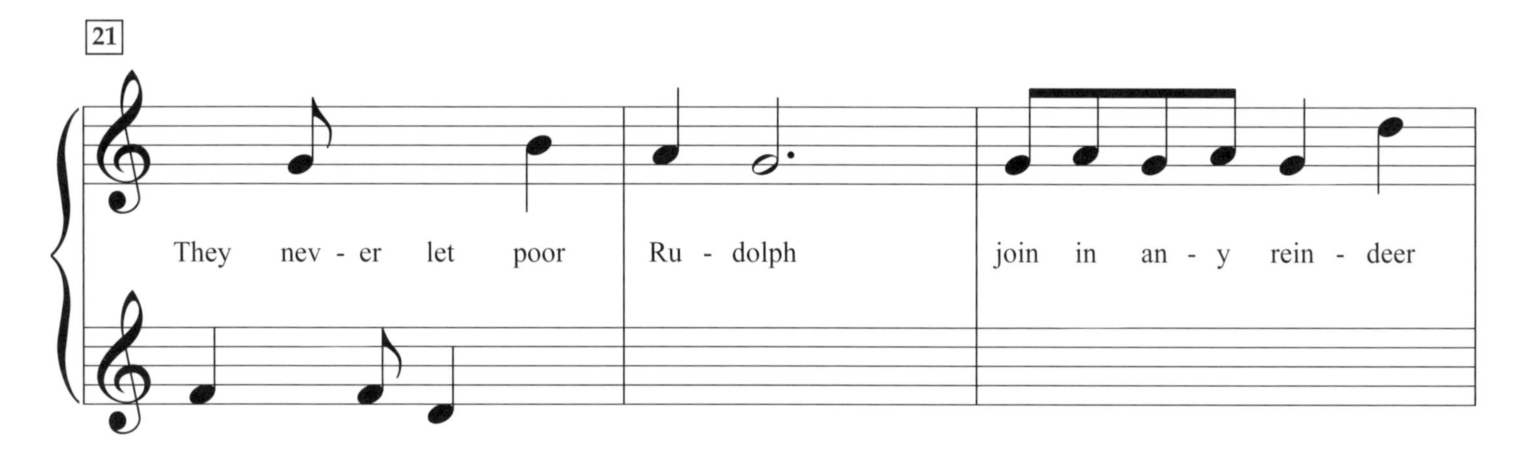
21
They nev - er let poor
Ru - dolph
join in an - y rein - deer

15
18
21

24
games.
Then one fog - gy
Christ - mas Eve
2
27
San - ta came to
say,
"Ru - dolph, with your
30
nose so bright,
won't you guide my
sleigh to - night?"
24
27
30

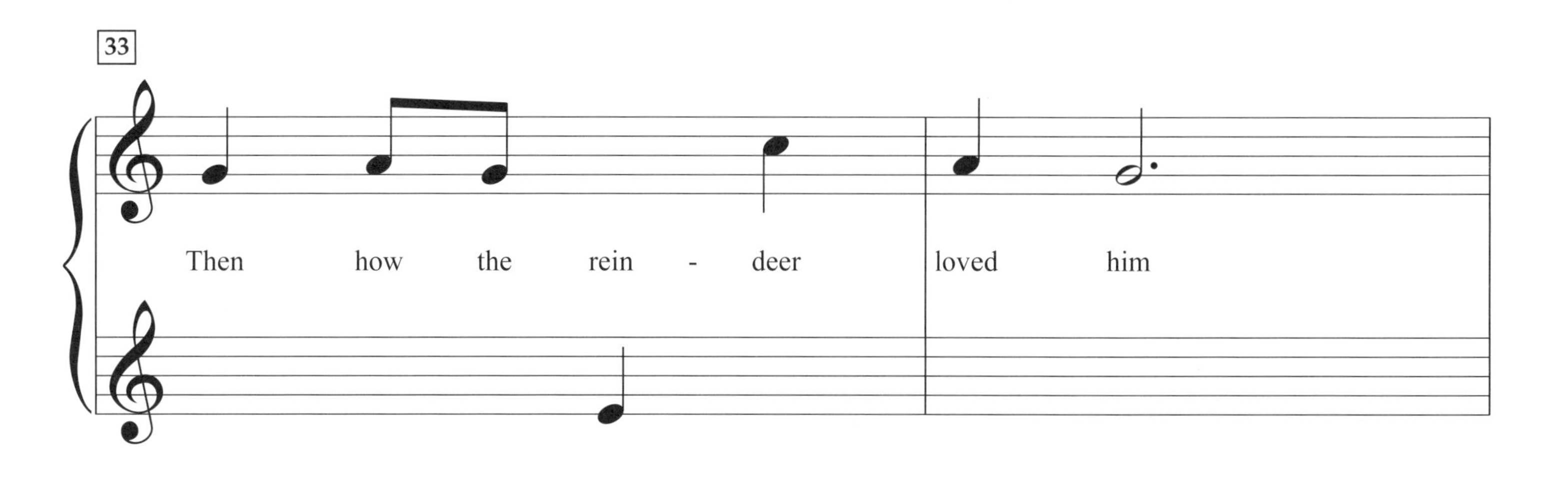
33
Then how the rein - deer loved him

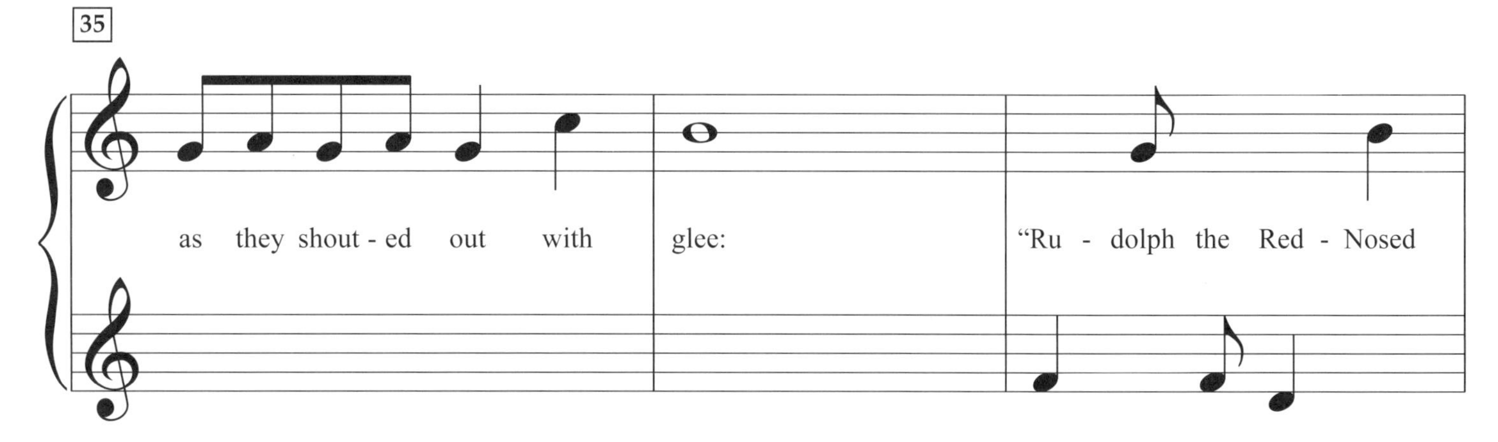
35
as they shout - ed out with glee:
glee:
"Ru - dolph the Red - Nosed

38
Rein - deer,
you'll go down in his - to - ry!"

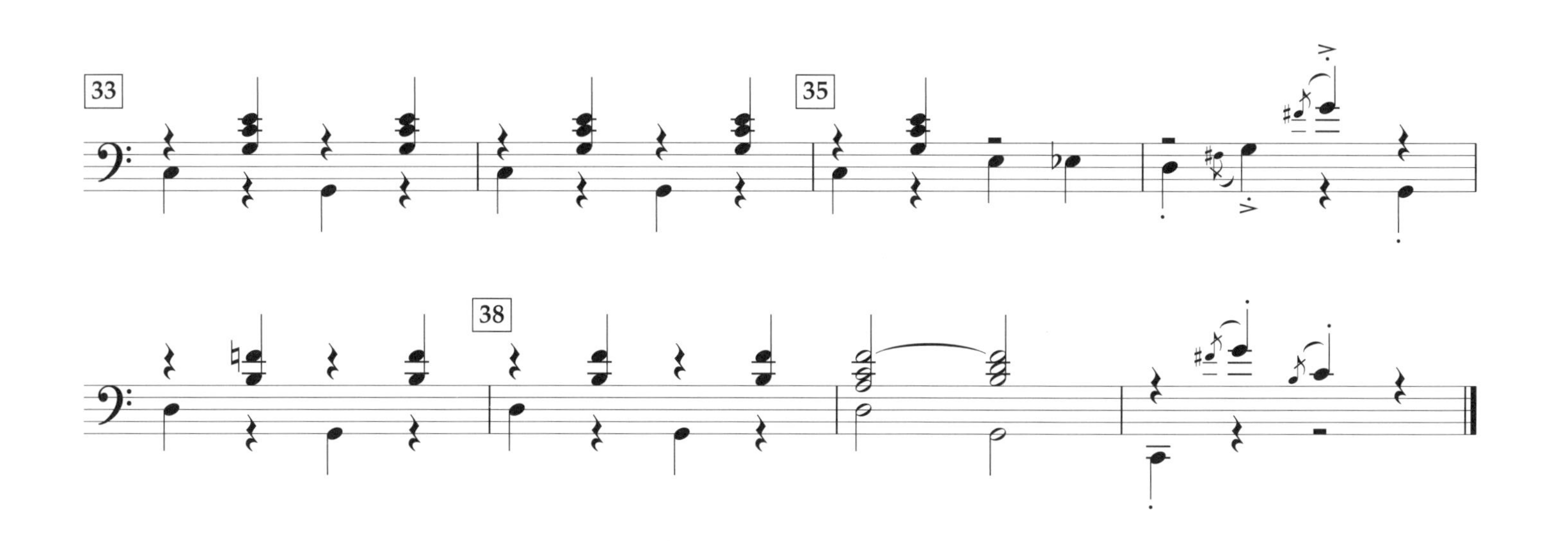
33
35
38

Silver and Gold

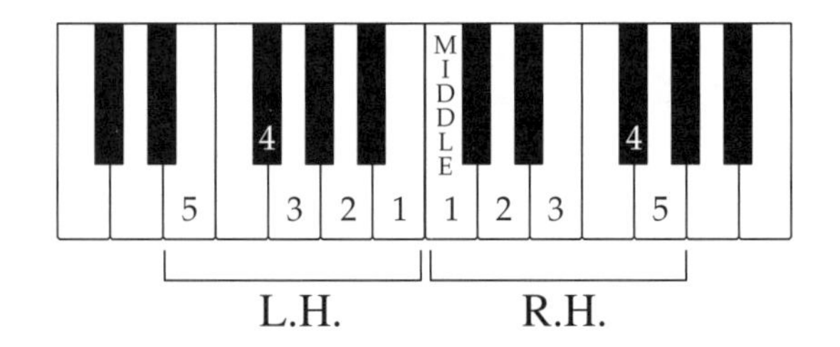

Music and Lyrics by
Johnny Marks

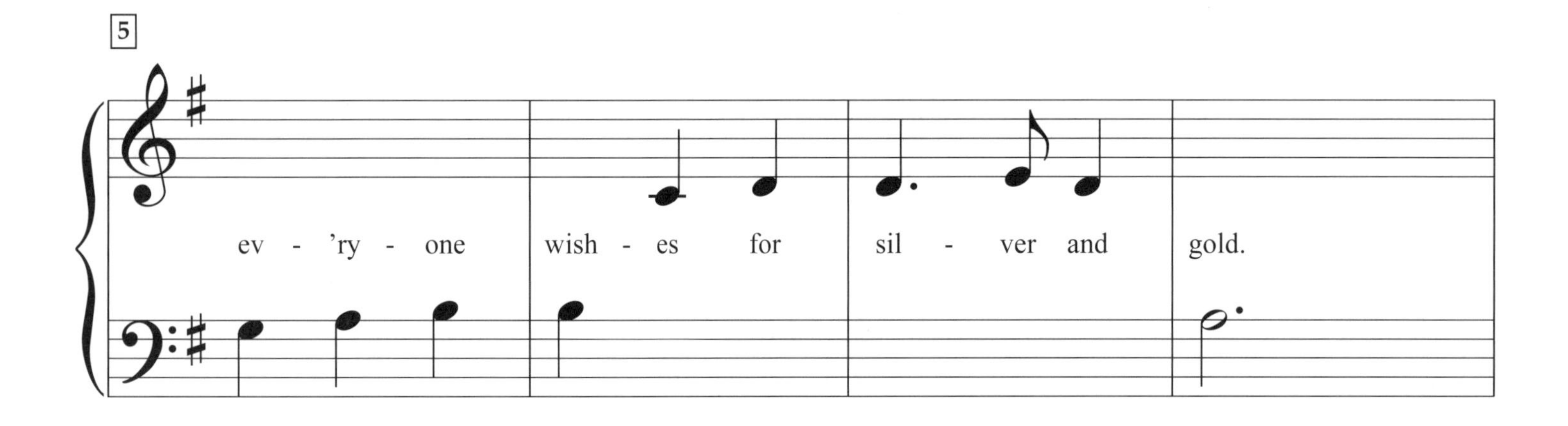

Duet Part (Student plays one octave higher than written.)

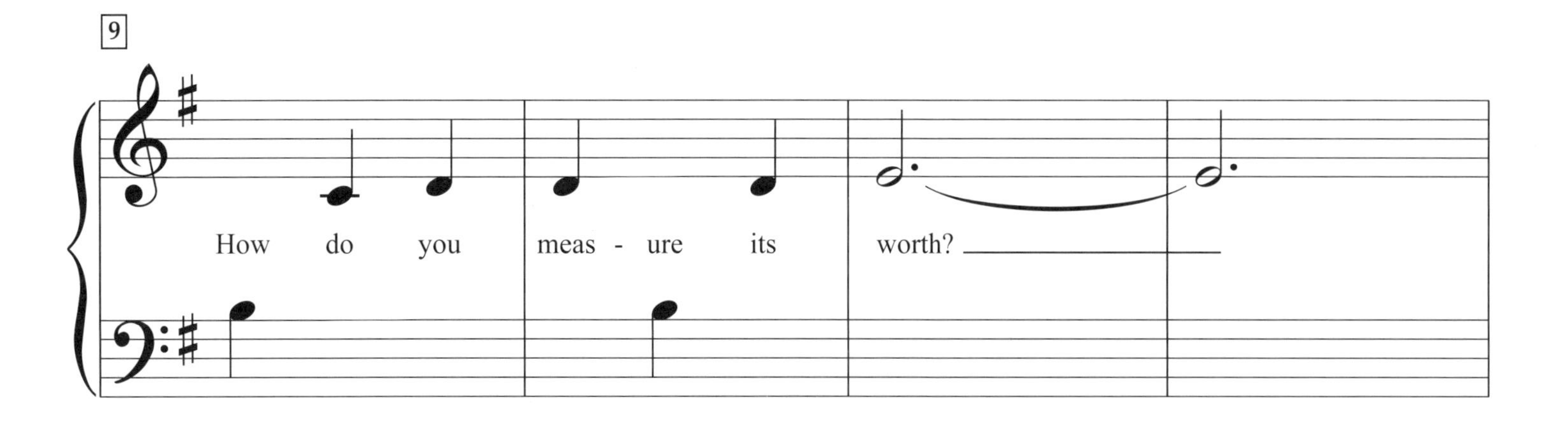
9
How do you meas - ure its worth?

13
Just by the pleas - ure it gives here on earth.
1

17
Sil - ver and gold, sil - ver and gold,

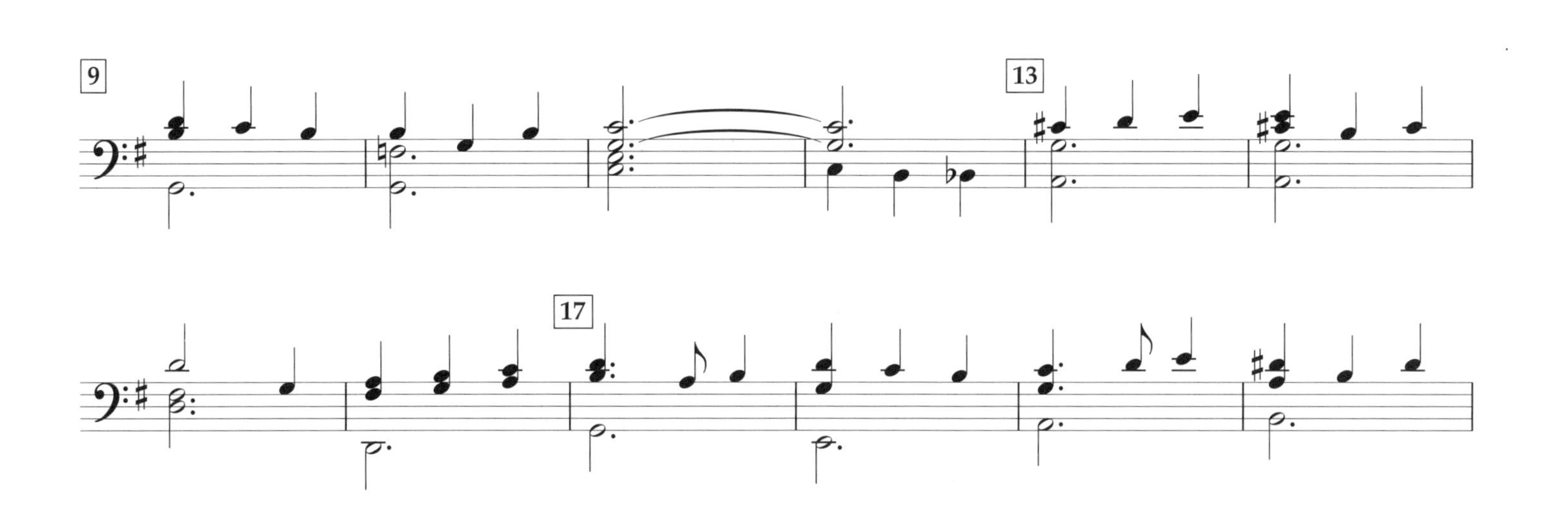
9
13
17

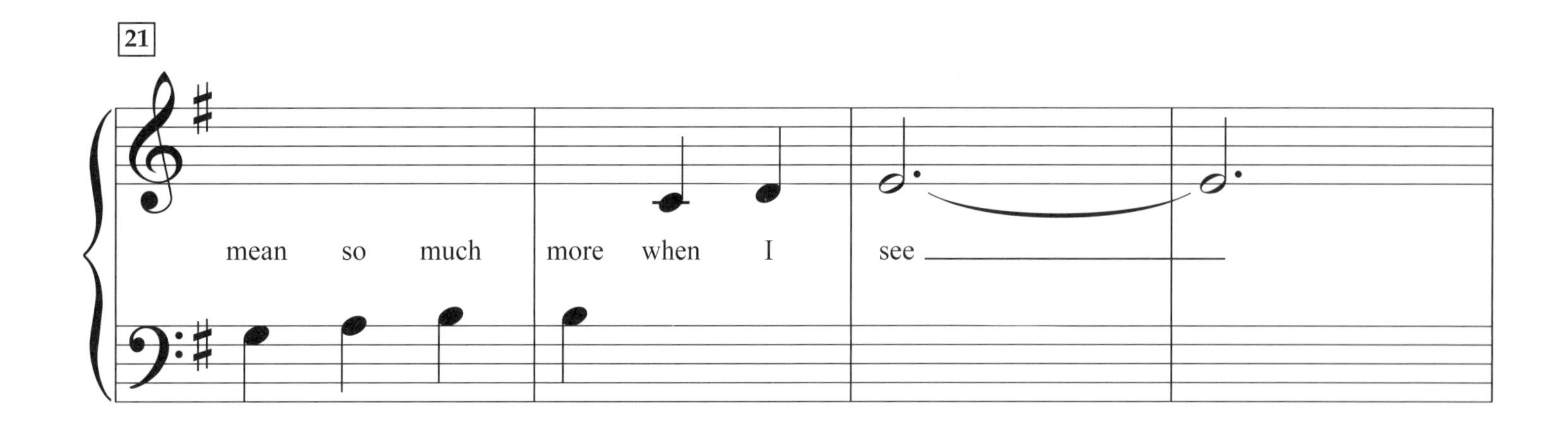
21
mean so much more when I see

25
sil - ver and gold dec - o - ra - tions on

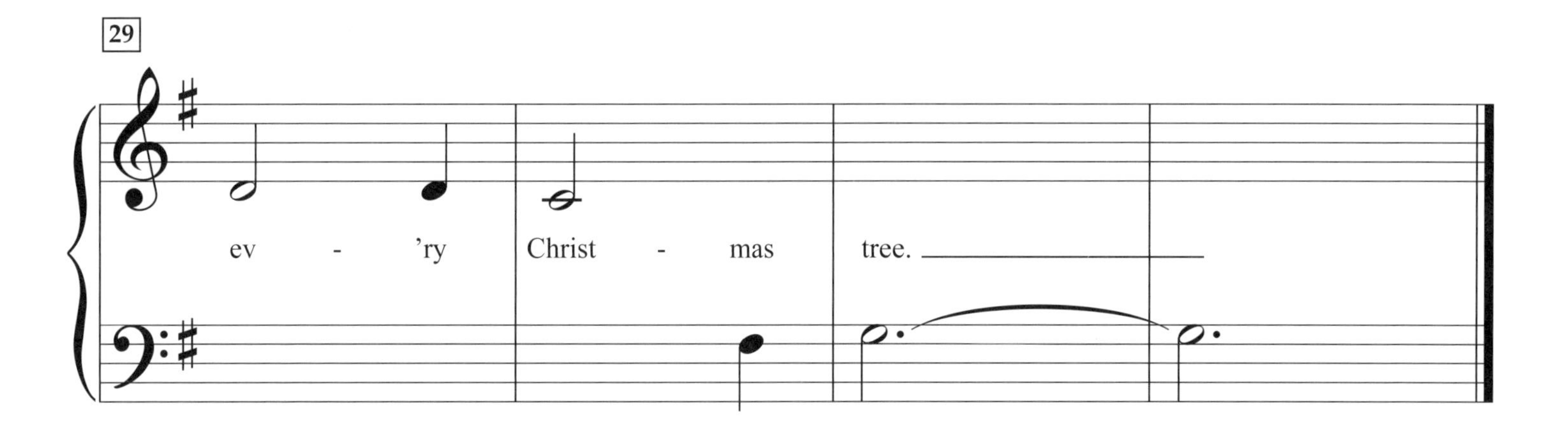
29
ev - 'ry Christ - mas tree.

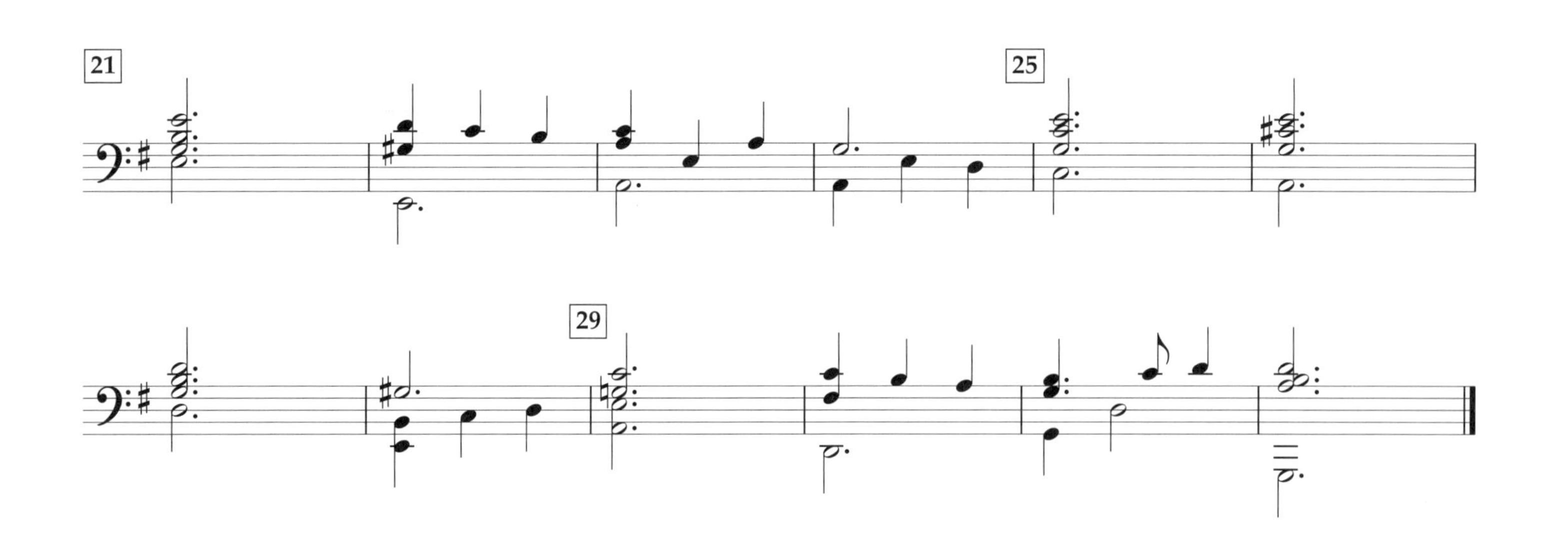
21
25
29

Where Are You Christmas?

from DR. SEUSS' HOW THE GRINCH STOLE CHRISTMAS

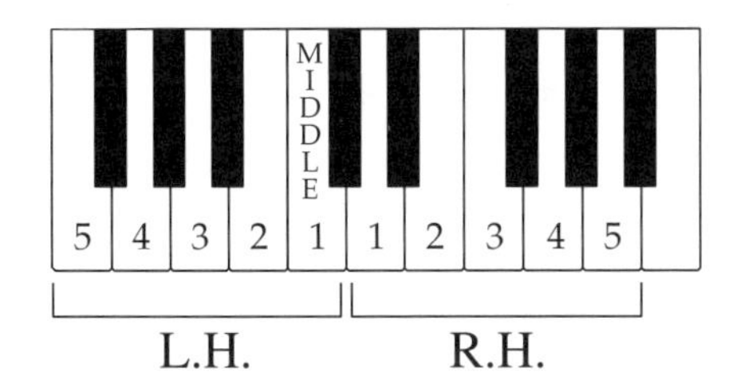

Words and Music by Will Jennings,
James Horner and Mariah Carey

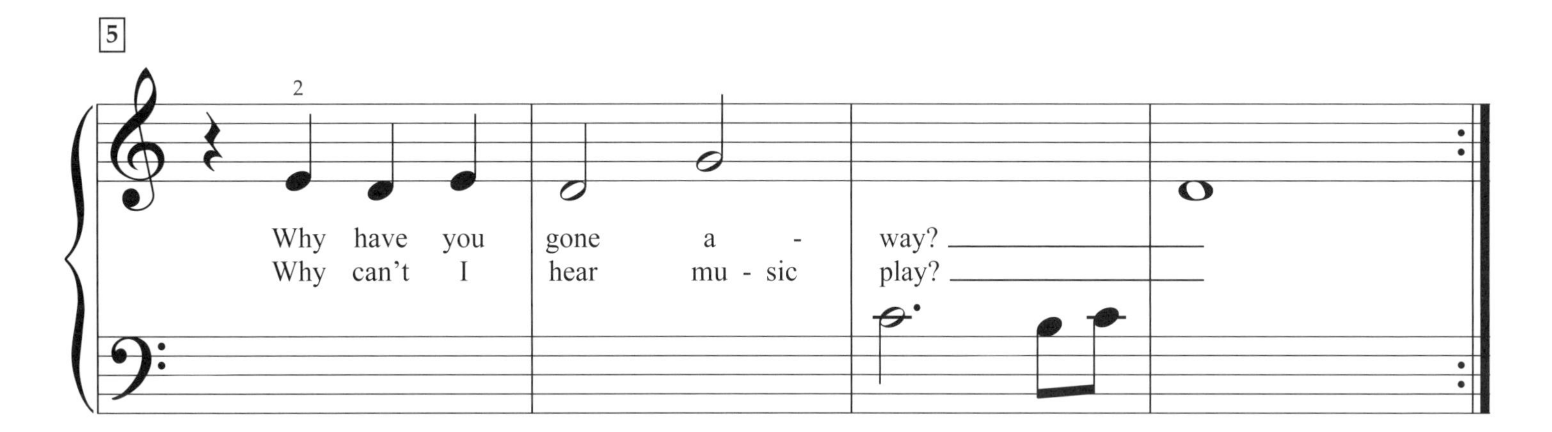

Duet Part (Student plays one octave higher than written.)

9
My world is chang - ing. ___ I'm re - ar - rang - ing.
1

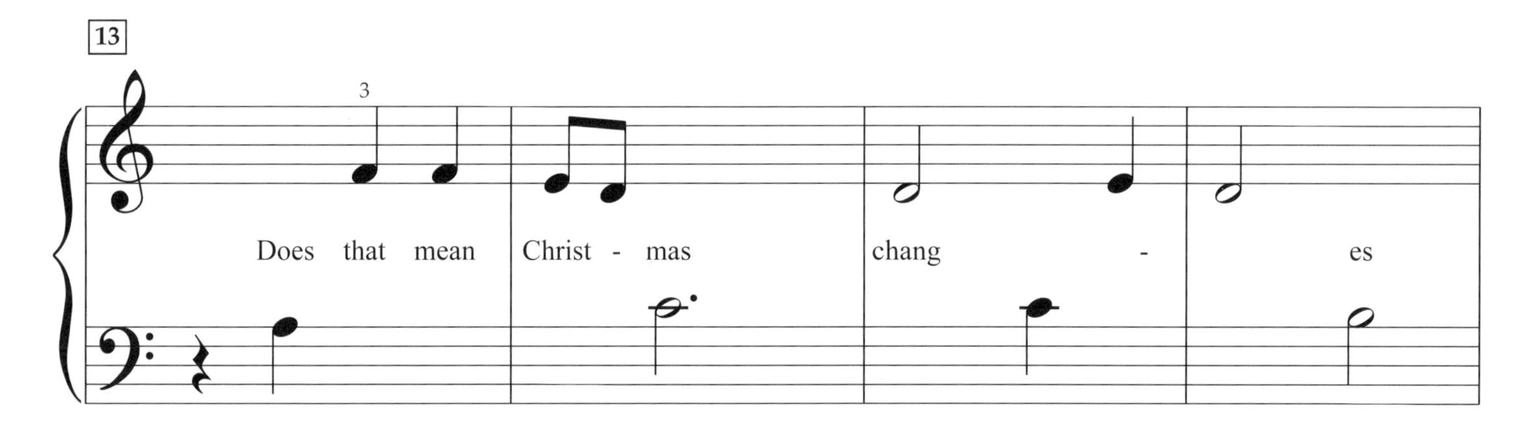
13
3
Does that mean Christ - mas chang - es

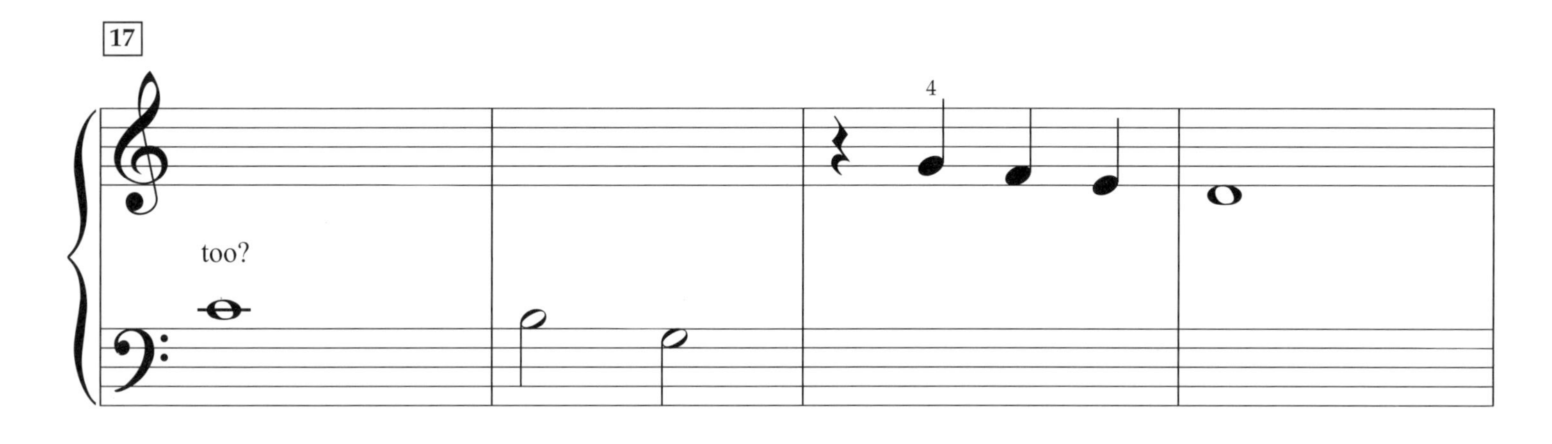
17
4
too?

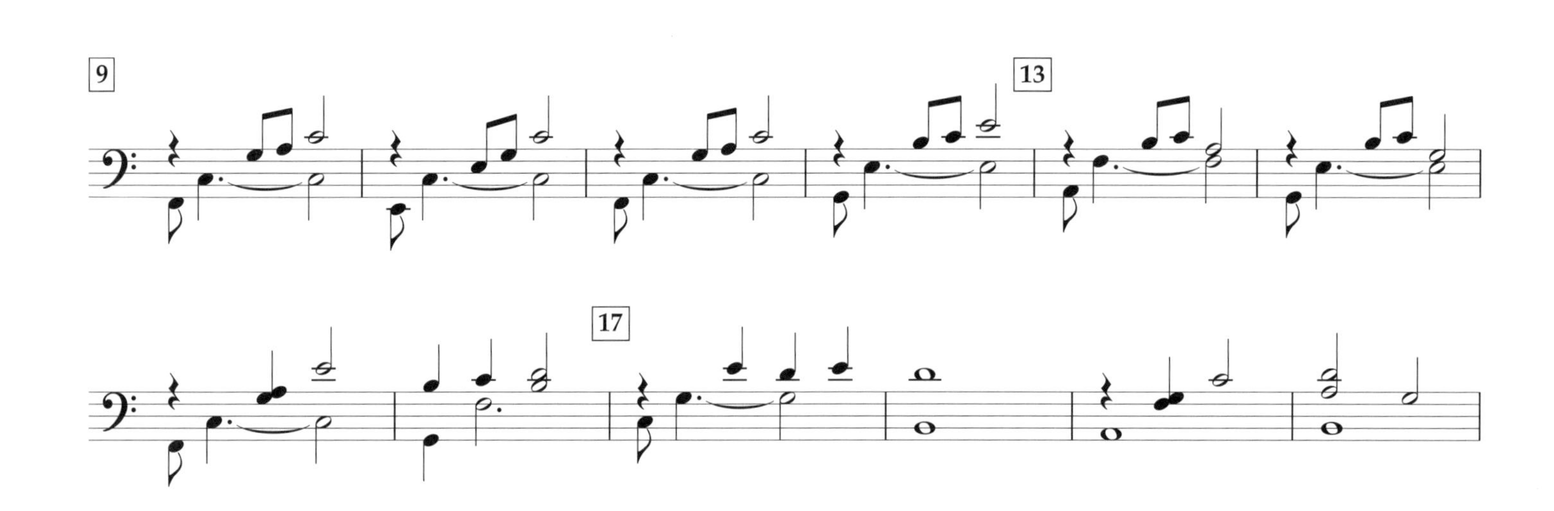
9
13
17

21
The joy of Christ - mas stays here in -

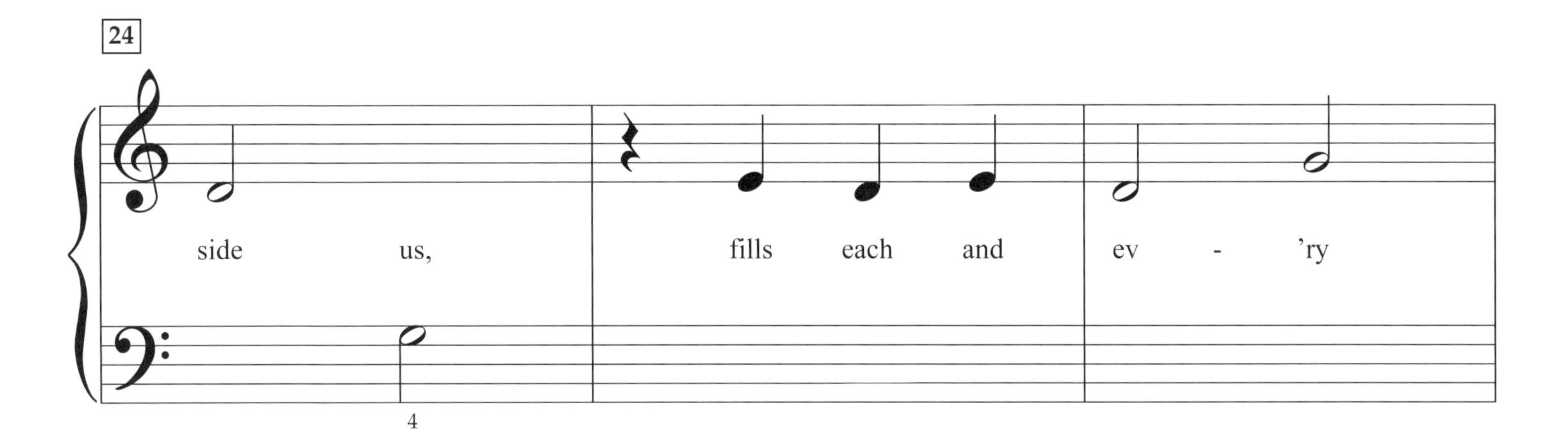
24
side us, fills each and ev - 'ry
4

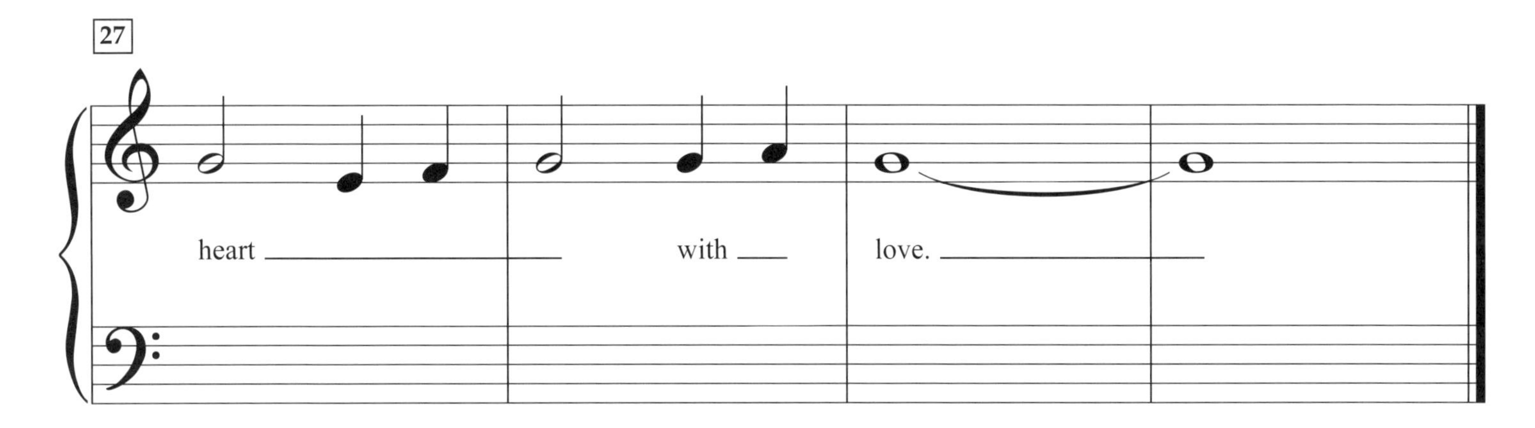
27
heart with love.

21
24

27

We Need a Little Christmas

from MAME

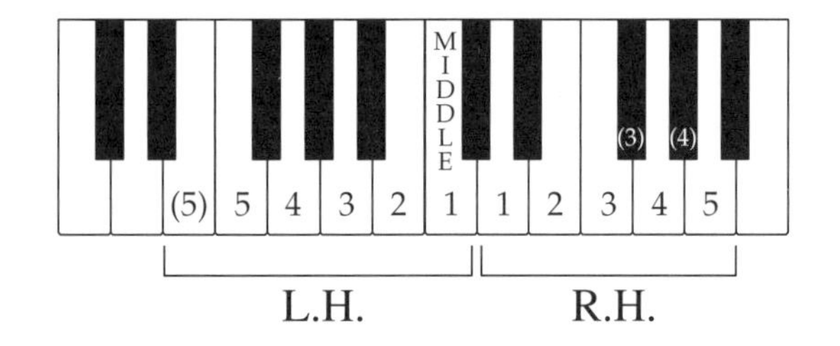

Music and Lyric by
Jerry Herman

Brightly

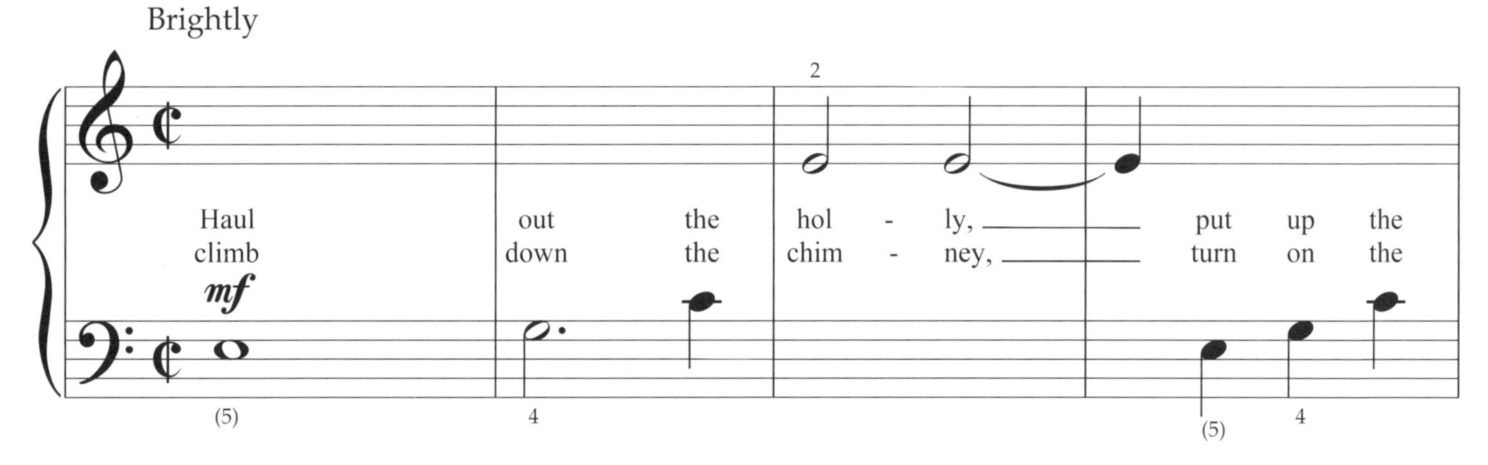

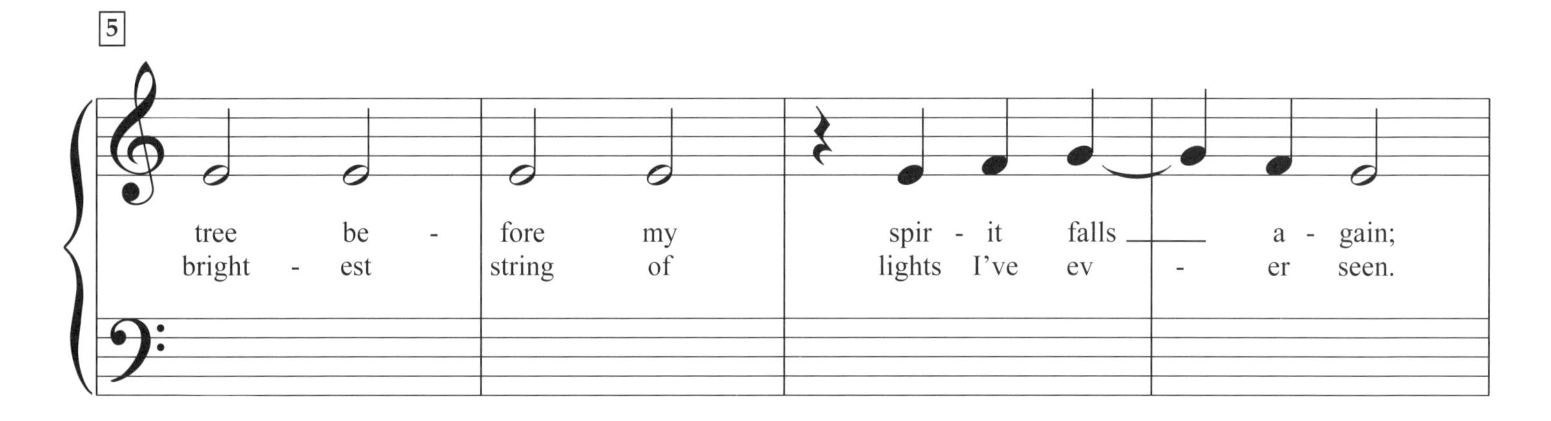

Duet Part (Student plays one octave higher than written.)

Brightly

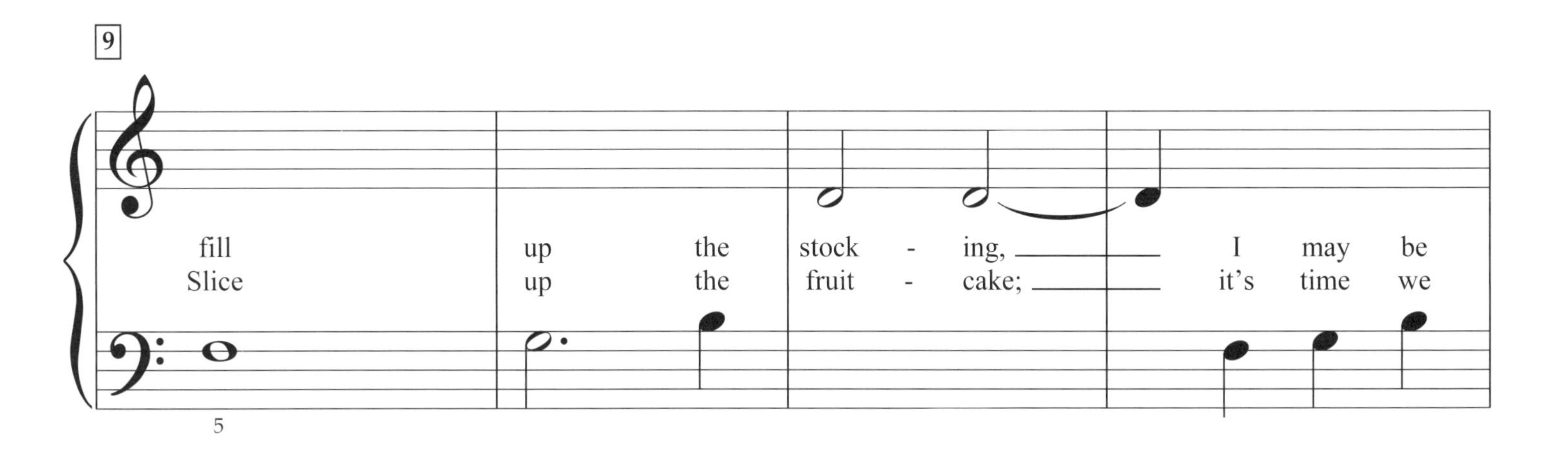
9
fill up the stock - ing, I may be
Slice up the fruit - cake; it's time we
5

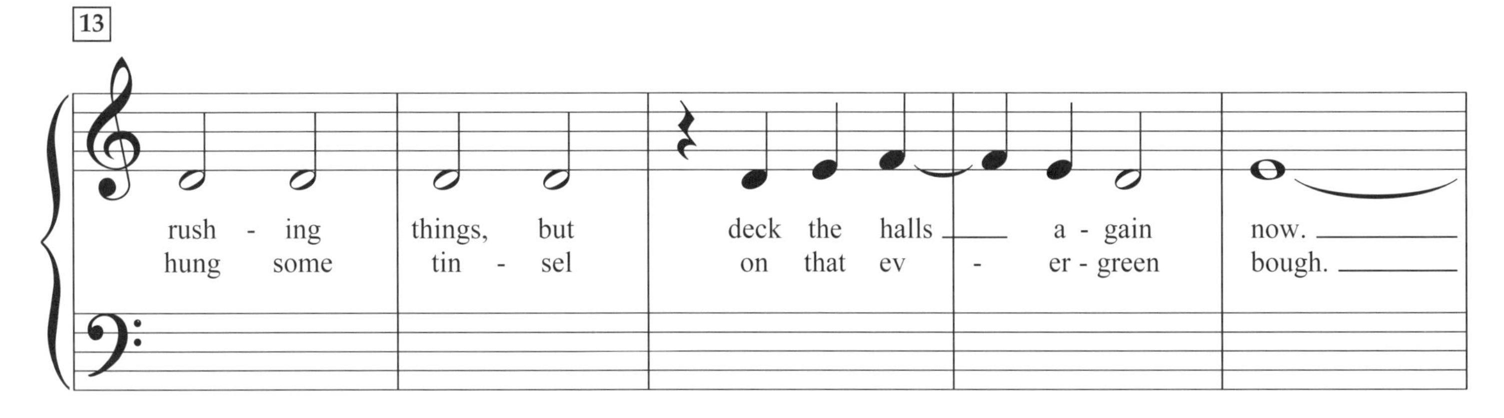
13
rush - ing things, but deck the halls a - gain now.
hung some tin - sel on that ev - er - green bough.

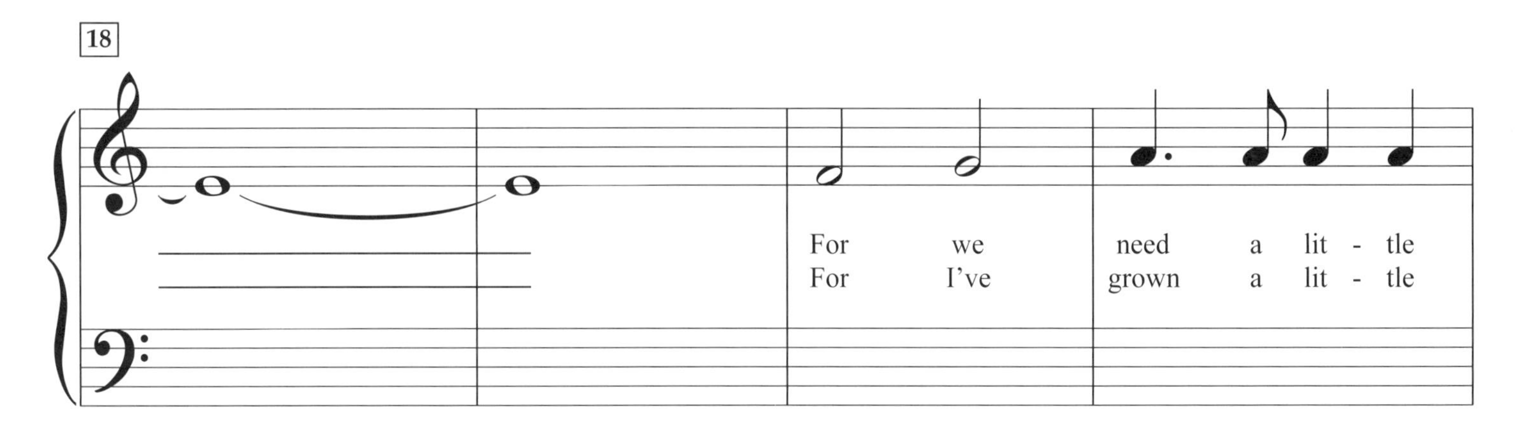
18
For we need a lit - tle
For I've grown a lit - tle

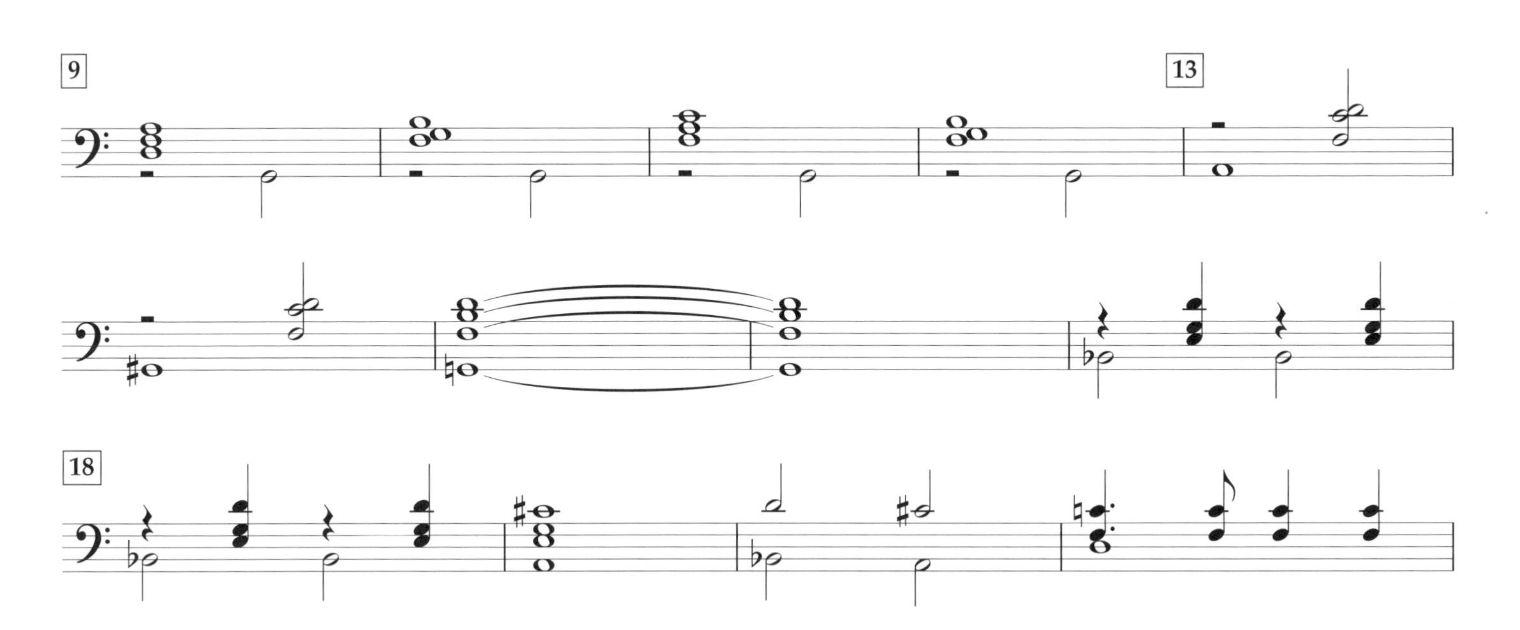
9
13
18

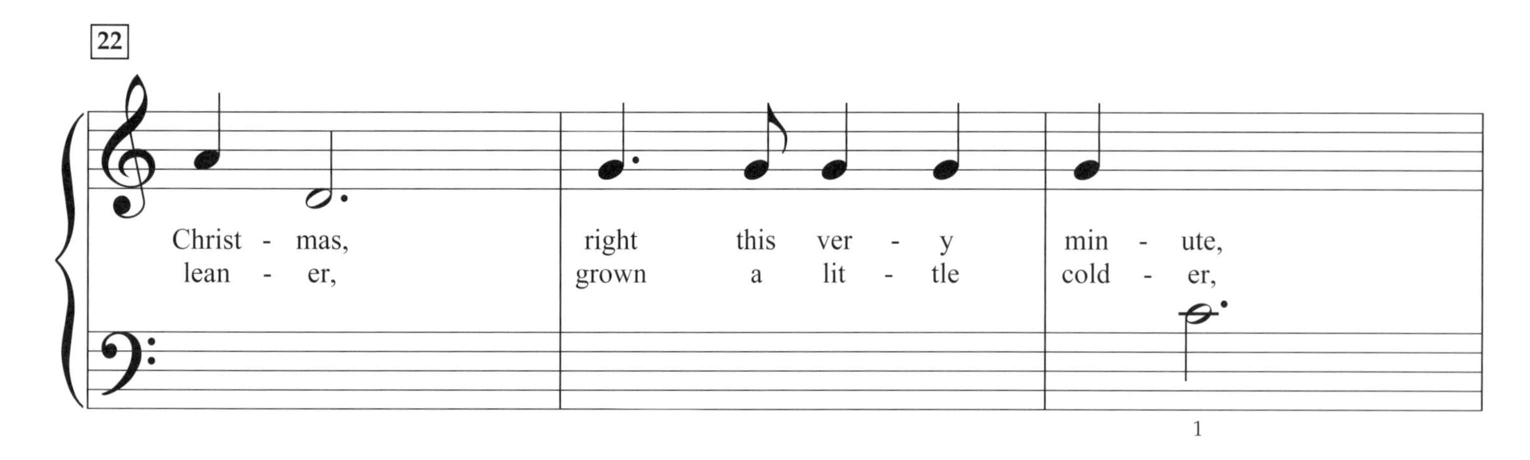
22
Christ - mas,
lean - er,
right this ver - y
grown a lit - tle
min - ute,
cold - er,
1
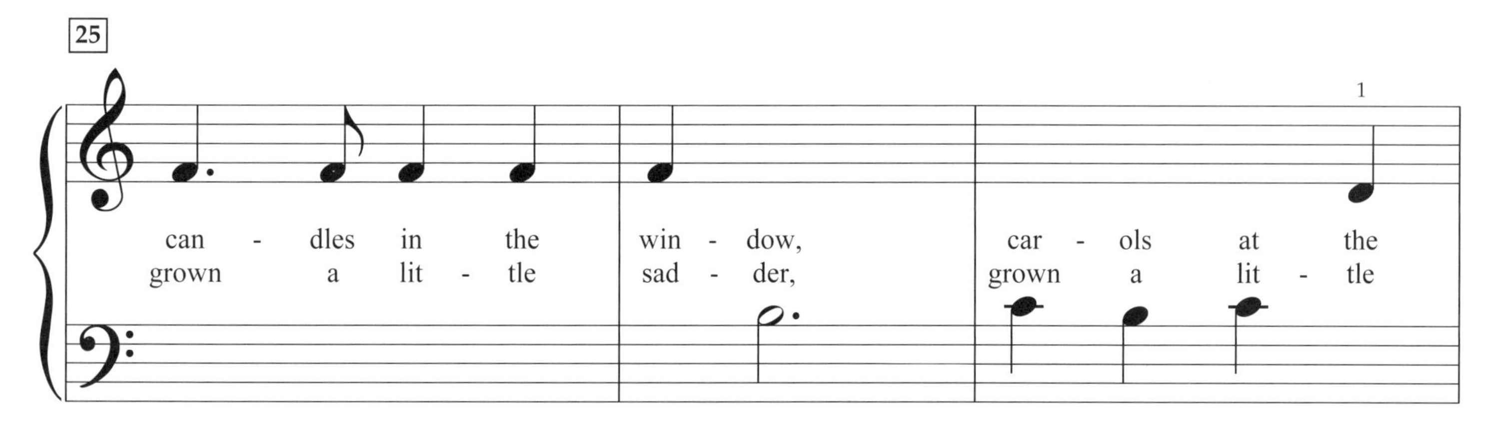
25
1
can - dles in the
grown a lit - tle
win - dow,
sad - der,
car - ols at the
grown a lit - tle
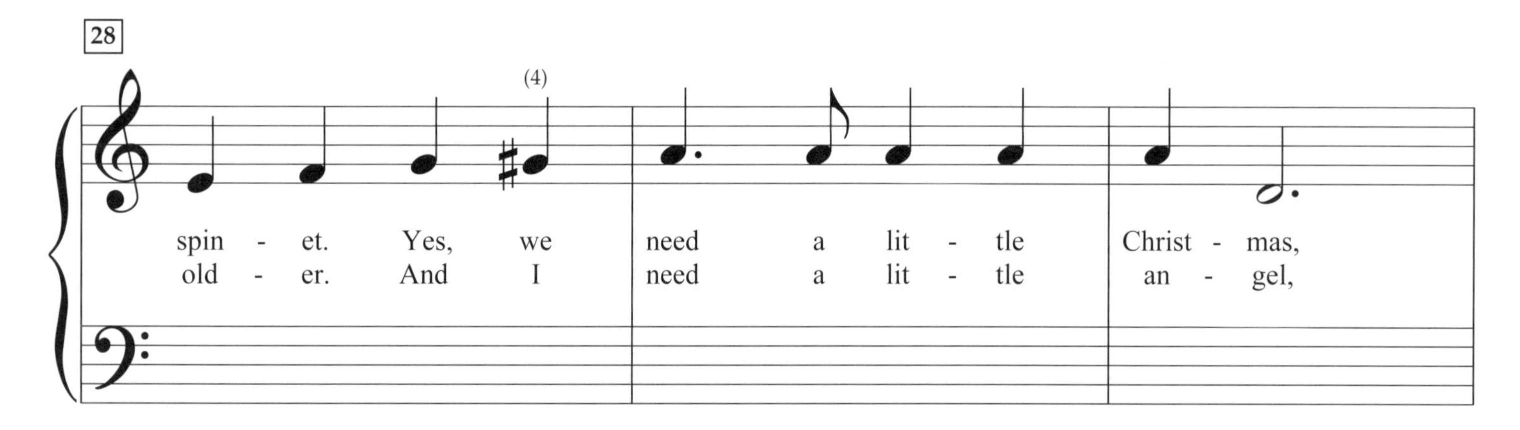
28
(4)
spin - et. Yes, we
old - er. And I
need a lit - tle
need a lit - tle
Christ - mas,
an - gel,
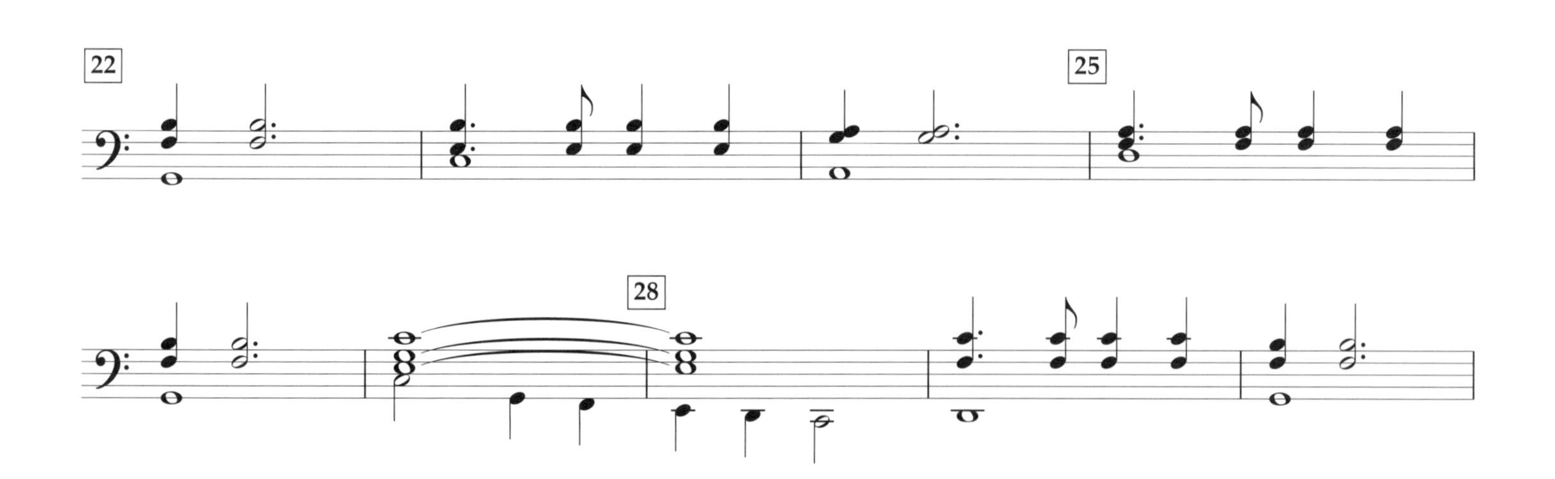
22
25
28

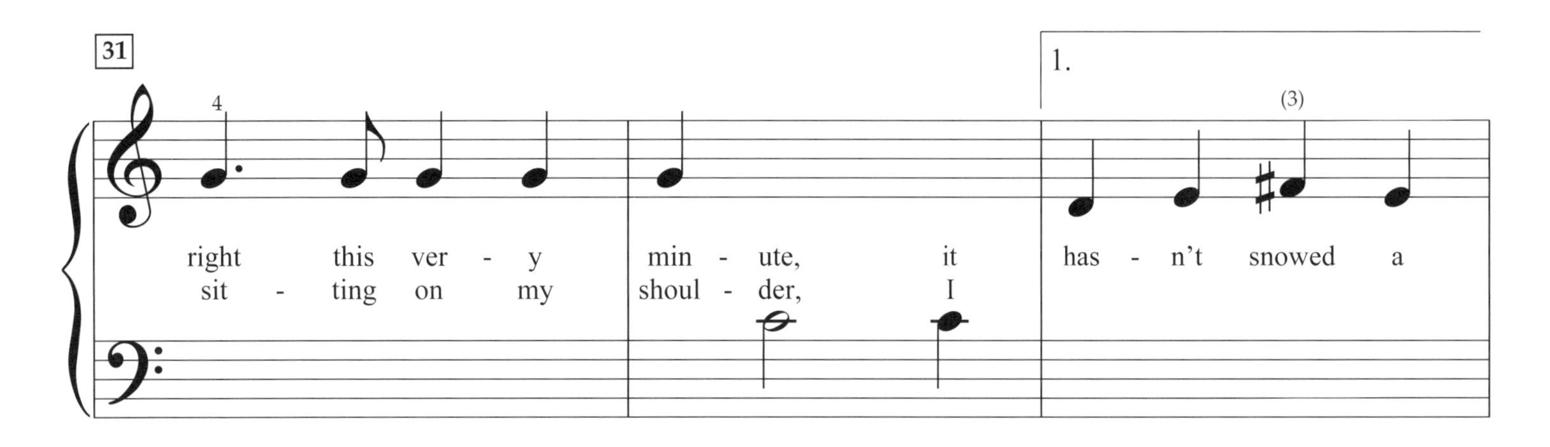
31
1.
4
(3)
right this ver - y min - ute, it has - n't snowed a
sit - ting on my shoul - der, I

34
sin - gle flur - ry, but San - ta, dear, we're in a hur - ry. So

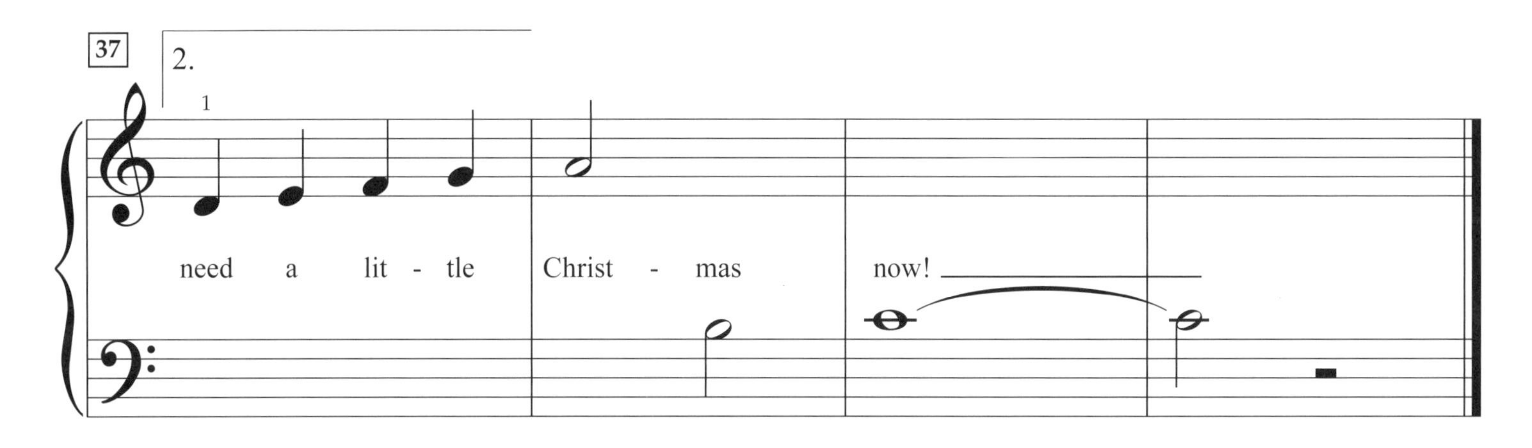
37
2.
1
need a lit - tle Christ - mas now!

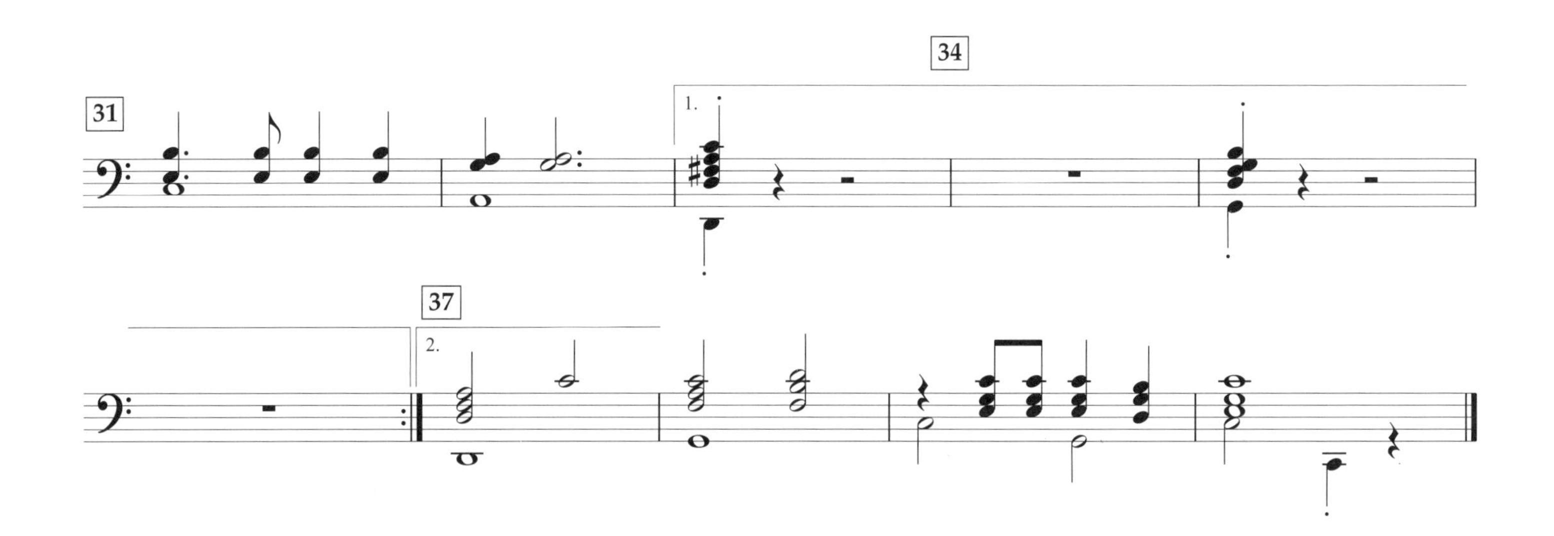
31
34
1.
37
2.